Reach Out

Student Book 3

Ben Wetz
Diana Pye

 CONTENTS

UNIT	VOCABULARY	LANGUAGE FOCUS
Starter unit	p4 Adjectives *easy, cheap, rare, useless*, etc.	p5 Comparative and superlative adjectives; Simple present **Key phrases:** Comparing

UNIT	VOCABULARY AND LANGUAGE FOCUS	READING	LANGUAGE FOCUS	VOCABULARY AND LISTENING
1 TV and news	p8–9 Television *show, advertisement, viewer, channel*, etc. **Key phrases:** Comparing opinions *was, were, there was, there were*	p10 Reality TV **Build your vocabulary:** Regular and irregular verbs	p11 Simple past	p12 On TV *drama series, documentary, reality show, chat show*, etc. **Study strategy:** Listening for specific information
Review: Unit 1 p16 Project: A TV program p17				
2 Disposable world	p18–19 Household goods *bottle, roll, carton, can*, etc. **Key phrases:** Saying numbers *much, many, a lot of, some, any*	p20 The "no impact" family **Study strategy:** Predicting **Build your vocabulary:** Compound nouns	p21 Relative pronouns	p22 Pollution and the environment *recycle, reuse, save, pollute*, etc.
Review: Unit 2 p26 Cumulative review: Starter–Unit 2 p27				
3 Life online	p28–29 The Internet *e-mail, instant messaging, file sharing*, etc. Present perfect: affirmative and negative	p30 Internet addiction **Study strategy:** Matching headings with paragraphs **Build your vocabulary:** Verb and noun collocations	p31 Present perfect: regular and irregular verbs	p32 Cybercrime *hacker, virus, password, firewall*, etc.
Review: Unit 3 p36 Project: A website plan p37				
4 Fame	p38–39 Adjectives: personality *friendly, sensitive, ambitious*, etc. Adverbs of degree **Study strategy:** Identifying cognates and false friends **Key phrases:** Describing people	p40 Celebrity culture **Build your vocabulary:** Prefixes and suffixes	p41 Present perfect + *still, yet, just*, and *already*	p42 Nouns and adjectives: personal qualities *style, stylish, skill, skillful*, etc. **Key phrases:** Talking about qualities
Review: Unit 4 p46 Cumulative review: Starter–Unit 4 p47				
5 School life	p48–49 School life: verbs *get good grades, pass tests, be truant*, etc. *should, must*, and *may not*	p50 Cheating **Build your vocabulary:** American vs. British English **Key phrases:** Agreeing and disagreeing	p51 *have to* and *don't have to*	p52 School life: nouns *coed schools, single-sex schools, public schools*, etc.
Review: Unit 5 p56 Project: A survey p57				
6 Take action	p58–59 Action and protest *publicize, campaign, boycott*, etc. **Key phrases:** Making suggestions *will* and *might*	p60 The food waste scandal **Build your vocabulary:** Negative prefixes: *un-, im-*, and *in-*	p61 First conditional	p62 Phrasal verbs: a campaign *look after, wipe out, carry on, end up*, etc. **Study strategy:** Making your own examples
Review: Unit 6 p66 Cumulative review: Starter–Unit 6 p67				
7 Movies and fiction	p68–69 Books and movies: genres *comedy, thriller, drama*, etc. Verbs + *-ing/to* **Key phrases:** Expressing likes and dislikes	p70 Movie technology **Study strategy:** Finding specific information **Build your vocabulary:** Suffixes: *-er* and *-or*	p71 *could, can, will be able to*	p72 Books and movies: features *beginning, ending, special effects, setting*, etc.
Review: Unit 7 p76 Project: A movie poster p77				
8 Art	p78–79 Nouns: art *painting, sculpture, gallery, portrait*, etc. Present passive: affirmative and negative	p80 Dada **Build your vocabulary:** Synonyms	p81 Past passive: affirmative and negative	p82 Adjectives: describing art *beautiful, controversial, amusing, shocking*, etc. **Study strategy:** Marking word stress
Review: Unit 8 p86 Cumulative review: Starter–Unit 8 p87				
Reach Out Options: p88 Extra listening and speaking; p96 Curriculum extra; p104 Culture; p112 Vocabulary bank				

VOCABULARY	LANGUAGE FOCUS
p6 Routines *do my homework, get home, go to sleep*, etc. **Key phrases:** Time words	p7 Present tenses

LANGUAGE FOCUS	SPEAKING	WRITING	REACH OUT OPTIONS
p13 Past tenses	p14 My news **Key phrases:** Talking about news	p15 A news article **Key phrases:** Writing a news item **Language point:** Time connectors	p88 **Extra listening and speaking:** Deciding what to watch on TV p96 **Curriculum extra:** Technology: Television p104 **Culture:** Television in the U.S. p112 **Vocabulary bank:** Regular and irregular verbs; TV and DVDs
p23 *too, too much, too many, enough, not enough*	p24 Offering and asking for help **Key phrases:** Offering and asking for help	p25 An environmental problem **Key phrases:** Writing an e-mail **Language point:** *so* and *because*	p89 **Extra listening and speaking:** Explaining what you want to buy p97 **Curriculum extra:** Geography: Sustainable development p105 **Culture:** Clean Up the World p113 **Vocabulary bank:** Compound nouns; Waste
p33 Present perfect: questions **Key phrases:** Experiences	p34 Apologizing and explaining **Key phrases:** Apologizing and explaining	p35 A comment on a website **Key phrases:** Expressing opinions **Language point:** Addition and contrast linkers	p90 **Extra listening and speaking:** Talking about websites p98 **Curriculum extra:** Technology: The Internet – wikis p106 **Culture:** Social networks around the world p114 **Vocabulary bank:** Verb and noun collocations; Personal details
p43 *for* and *since*; Present perfect and simple past	p44 Identifying and describing people **Key phrases:** Identifying people	p45 A biography **Key phrases:** A biography **Language point:** Order of adjectives	p91 **Extra listening and speaking:** Describing people p99 **Curriculum extra:** Language and literature: Newspapers p107 **Culture:** Teenage magazines p115 **Vocabulary bank:** Prefixes and suffixes; Music
p53 *should, must,* and *have to* **Study strategy:** Improving your English	p54 Asking for and giving advice **Key phrases:** Asking for and giving advice	p55 An opinion essay **Key phrases:** Expressing opinions **Language point:** Ordering information	p92 **Extra listening and speaking:** Talking about your school p100 **Curriculum extra:** Citizenship: The school community p108 **Culture:** Studying abroad p116 **Vocabulary bank:** American vs. British English; School
p63 *be going to* and *will* Plans and predictions; Intentions and instant decisions	p64 Plans and arrangements **Key phrases:** Donating money **Language point:** Present continuous for future arrangements	p65 A formal letter **Key phrases:** Formal letters **Language point:** Explaining	p93 **Extra listening and speaking:** Interviewing a campaigner p101 **Curriculum extra:** Geography: Natural environments p109 **Culture:** Charities: Comic Relief p117 **Vocabulary bank:** Negative prefixes: *un-, im-,* and *in-*; The environment
p73 Second conditional	p74 Expressing preferences and recommending **Key phrases:** Recommending and responding	p75 A review of a book or a movie **Key phrases:** Facts and opinions **Language point:** Paragraphs and topic sentences	p94 **Extra listening and speaking:** Interviewing someone about a movie p102 **Curriculum extra:** Language and literature: Word building – nouns p110 **Culture:** The British movie industry p118 **Vocabulary bank:** Suffixes: *-er* and *-or*; Filmmaking
p83 Present and past passive: affirmative, negative, and questions **Key phrases:** Doing a quiz	p84 Expressing doubt **Key phrases:** Describing art	p85 A description of a piece of art **Key phrases:** Describing a painting **Language point:** Using synonyms	p95 **Extra listening and speaking:** Discussing a picture p103 **Curriculum extra:** Visual arts: Art movements of the 20th century p111 **Culture:** Graffiti artists – past and present p119 **Vocabulary bank:** Synonyms; Works of art

Starter unit

VOCABULARY ■ Adjectives

I can use adjectives to talk about the world around me.

1 1.02 Match adjectives 1–12 with their opposites in the box. Then listen and check.

easy cheap rare useless near quiet unhealthy weak heavy clean exciting dangerous

1 expensive	5 safe	9 difficult
2 common	6 healthy	10 light
3 powerful	7 dirty	11 useful
4 noisy	8 far	12 boring

2 1.03 Work in pairs. Choose the correct words in *The world around you* quiz. Then think of an answer for each description 1–6. Listen and check.

3 ACTIVATE Think of an example for 1–8. Then ask and answer with a partner.

It's an exciting sport. It begins with the letter "b."

Is it basketball?

1 an exciting sport	5 a dangerous animal
2 a powerful person	6 a common material
3 a healthy food	7 a difficult subject
4 a useful machine	8 a boring movie

Finished?

Write more quiz items with the adjectives in exercise 1.

You wear this when you want to be safe on your bike.

The world around you

1 This planet is the furthest from the Sun. It is further than Jupiter. It takes 165 Earth years to go around the Sun. Mercury is the nearest to the sun, but it's also the hottest. Earth is also pretty **safe** / **near** – a distance of about 149 million kilometers.

2 This city has a population of more than 13 million people. It's one of the biggest cities in the world and it's very **noisy** / **useful**. People don't speak English here.

3 This is a **rare** / **common** insect and it's also one of the most dangerous because it causes malaria. It doesn't live in cold countries and it loves dirty water.

4 These animals are **difficult** / **powerful** and intelligent. They have the heaviest brains in the animal kingdom. They eat fish. A newborn baby is over 500 kg!

5 This is one of the most common materials in houses around the world. It's **cheap** / **healthy** and useful. We make it from oil.

6 This metal is heavier than gold and it's also rarer and more **clean** / **expensive**. It has a silver-white color and it costs about $50,000 per kilo. We make jewelry with it.

I can make comparisons and talk about things that people do.

Comparative and superlative adjectives

1 Complete the tables with adjectives from the quiz on page 4. Then answer questions 1–3.

Comparative adjectives
Platinum is heavier than gold and it's also [1]___.
Platinum is more [2]___.
Neptune is [3]___ than Jupiter.

Superlative adjectives
Mercury is the [4]___ to the sun. It's also the [5]___.
Plastic is one of the most [6]___ materials.
Neptune is the [7]___ from the sun.

1 What are the rules for forming comparatives and superlatives of short adjectives?
2 What are the rules for forming comparatives and superlatives of long adjectives?
3 Which adjective is irregular?

More practice ⇨ Workbook page 5

2 Write a comparative and superlative sentence for each group of words.

a vacation, a test, a DVD (exciting)
A DVD is more exciting than a test. A vacation is the most exciting.

1 a koala, a leopard, a horse (slow)
2 cars, video games, magazines (expensive)
3 burgers, candy, soda (bad for you)
4 train, plane, car (dangerous)
5 nightclubs, supermarkets, libraries (noisy)

3 Study the key phrases. Then talk about 1–4 with a partner.

KEY PHRASES ○ Comparing

much	better than
a little / a lot	more interesting than
not	as interesting as
twice / three times	as good as

I think that the Chicago Bulls are the best basketball team.

I disagree. I think that the Los Angeles Lakers are much better than the Bulls.

1 team (good)
2 book (interesting)
3 school subject (easy)
4 language (useful)

Simple present

4 Complete the sentences from the quiz on page 4. How does the verb change in the third person singular?

1 We ___ jewelry with it.
2 People ___ English here.
3 It ___ dirty water.
4 It ___ in cold countries.

More practice ⇨ Workbook page 5

5 Complete the table using the third person singular of the verbs in the box.

~~finish~~ do watch study relax
go try pass teach carry

Verbs ending in *-o*, *-x*, *-ss*, *-ch*, *-sh* → + *-es*	Verbs ending in consonant + *-y* → ~~y~~ + *-ies*
finish – finishes	

6 Write affirmative sentences (✔), negative sentences (✘), and questions (?).

1 My parents (work) in Boston. ✔
2 We (eat lunch) at school. ✘
3 You (go) to a swimming club. ?
4 My brother (get) up early. ✔
5 He (make) his bed. ✘
6 Your friend (talk) to you. ?
7 She (eat breakfast) on school days. ✘
8 Your mother (take) the bus to work. ?

7 ACTIVATE Write six questions about the things in the table. Then interview your partner.

How often When Where What time	do does	you your friends your teacher your mom your dad	go to the movies do your homework do the dishes work play soccer cook get up watch TV

When do you do your homework?

On the weekend. What about you?

○ *Finished?*
Write five sentences about your partner using the ideas in exercise 7.
He sometimes does the dishes on the weekend.

VOCABULARY ■ Routines

I can talk about routines and say when I do things.

1 1.04 **Complete the text with the phrases in the box. Then listen and check your answers.**

are you doing start do my homework go to sleep watch TV 's buying get home get the bus wakes 're looking go to bed aren't playing relax go shopping get up ~~'m interviewing~~ eat breakfast goes to work 'm waiting finishes

Katie Excuse me. I'*m interviewing* students about their typical day. Can I ask you some questions, please?
Lily Sure, I'm not busy. I [1]___ for my brother. He [2]___ sneakers in that store. Are you doing interviews for a magazine?
Katie That's right, a student magazine. What [3]___ at the mall this morning?
Lily We [4]___ for a present for our mom.
Katie Do you always [5]___ on Saturdays?
Lily No, I don't. I usually go to basketball on Saturday mornings, but we [6]___ today. My brother isn't playing soccer today, either.
Katie Now about your day. What time do you [7]___ in the morning?
Lily That depends on the day. My mom [8]___ me up at 7:00, before she [9]___, but I don't get up immediately. I sometimes [10]___ again.
Katie Do you [11]___?
Lily I have a quick piece of toast or some cereal. Then my brother and I [12]___ to school. My brother finishes his homework on the bus. He isn't very organized.
Katie What time does school [13]___?
Lily School starts at 8:30 and [14]___ at 3:30.
Katie Do you usually go straight home after school?
Lily Usually, yes. And I like to [15]___ when I [16]___. After that, I can relax.
Katie How do you [17]___?
Lily I go on the computer and chat, or [18]___ if there's something good on.
Katie And what time do you [19]___?
Lily At 10:00, in theory, but my parents aren't too strict. My brother goes to bed earlier because he's younger.

2 **Work in pairs. Look at the pictures in this book and say true or false sentences about them. Use the present continuous.**

On page twenty-one, a man is riding his bike with four children.

False.

3 **Write one thing you do at each of these times. Compare your answers with a partner.**

After I wake up, I check what time it is.

1 After you wake up.
2 After you get up.
3 Before you go to school.
4 Before school starts.
5 When school finishes.
6 When you get home.
7 Before you go to bed.
8 Before you go to sleep.

4 ACTIVATE **Study the key phrases. Then talk about your routines with a partner. Use the key phrases, the activities in exercise 1, or your own ideas.**

KEY PHRASES ○ Time words

on Thursdays / Thursday evenings
on the weekend / at night /
at (about) seven o'clock
in the morning / afternoon / evening
once or twice a day / week / month
every Friday

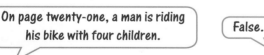

I go to bed at nine o'clock.

Oh? I go to bed at ten o'clock!

LANGUAGE FOCUS ■ Present tenses

I can talk about things happening now and repeated actions.

Present continuous

1 Complete the tables. Then look at the dialogue on page 6 and check.

Affirmative
I [1]___ waiting for my brother.
We [2]___ looking for a present for our mom.

Negative
We [3]___ playing today.
My brother [4]___ playing soccer today.

Questions
What [5]___ you doing at the mall?
[6]___ you doing interviews for a magazine?

More practice ⇨ Workbook page 7

2 Complete the sentences with the present continuous form of the verbs in the box.

eat not play not wear not smile
study watch

1 They're in the kitchen. They ___ breakfast.
2 She ___ right now. She isn't happy.
3 I ___ that because I don't like pink.
4 Dave ___ soccer because he has a bad leg.
5 We ___ a great movie.
6 My sister ___ for a test.

3 Write questions for the answers.

Who (call)? She's calling Sue.
Who's she calling?
1 (study)? No, they aren't.
2 Why (cry)? Because she's upset.
3 Where (go)? I'm going to the movies.
4 (joke)? Yes, he is.
5 What (do)? We're watching a DVD.
6 Who (hug)? She's hugging her son.

Simple present and present continuous

4 Complete the table with sentences a–c. Which sentences are in the simple present and which are in the present continuous?

a They chat every day.
b I sometimes eat in a restaurant.
c I'm eating in a restaurant right now.

Action happening now	Routine or repeated action
They're talking on the phone. [1]___	[2]___ [3]___

More practice ⇨ Workbook page 7

5 Complete the dialogue with the simple present or present continuous form of the verbs in parentheses.

Mark Hey, Jenny. Why are you standing there? [1]___ (you / watch) someone?
Jenny Yes, look – Mandy and Shaun [2]___ (talk).
Mark Oh, yes, and Mandy [3]___ (smile). What [4]___ (they / say)?
Jenny I'm not sure. I can't hear.
Mark Shaun never [5]___ (speak) to Mandy.
Jenny Yes, he does. He sometimes [6]___ (joke) with her in class.
Mark He [7]___ (leave) now, but she [8]___ (not go) with him.
Jenny Mmm. Very interesting!

6 ACTIVATE Work in pairs. Ask and answer questions. Use the verbs, nouns, and time expressions in the table, or your own ideas.

Verbs	Nouns	Time expressions
do	you	never
get up	the teacher	right now
go	this exercise	after school
speak	to school	in the morning
walk	your homework	now
listen	music	on the weekend
play	computer games	every day

1 TV and news

Start thinking

1 What's a reality show?
2 How much TV do you watch?
3 What are the most popular TV programs in your country?

Aims

Communication: I can ...

- exchange opinions about TV.
- understand a text about reality TV.
- talk about past events.
- understand and present news.
- talk about what people were doing.
- talk about my news.
- write a news item.

Vocabulary

- Television
- On TV

Language focus

- *was, were, there was, there were*
- Simple past
- Past continuous
- Simple past and past continuous

Reach Out Options

Extra listening and speaking

Deciding what to watch on TV

Page 88

Curriculum extra

Technology: Television

Page 96

Culture

Television in the U.S.

Page 104

Vocabulary bank

Regular and irregular verbs; TV and DVDs

Page 112

VOCABULARY AND LANGUAGE FOCUS ■ Television

I can exchange opinions about TV.

1 Study the words in blue in the *TV Quiz*. Then put them in the correct list.

Equipment	People	On TV
screen 1___ 2___	*audience* 3___ 4___ 5___ 6___	*episode* 7___ 8___ 9___ 10___ 11___ 12___

2 1.05 Do the *TV Quiz* with a partner. Then listen and check your answers.

3 1.06 Complete the key phrases with the words in the box. Then listen to the first part of the conversation again and check.

my so with sure don't think

KEY PHRASES ◯ Comparing opinions

I'm not 1___.
In 2___ opinion, (there are a lot).
I 3___ agree.
I think (the answer is "a").
I don't think 4___.
I agree 5___ you.
I 6___ so, too.

1 The biggest TV audiences last year were for ...
a sports programs.
b comedy shows.
c news programs.

2 In the U.S. in 1985, there were 19 channels. Now there are ...
a between 20 and 30.
b between 100 and 120.
c between 1,000 and 1,200.

3 For a long time, the Simpsons were the most popular comedy characters in the world. When was the first episode of *The Simpsons* on TV? Was it in ...
a 1979?
b 1999?
c 1989?

4 There was a historic TV broadcast in 1969. Why was it special?
a It was the first TV broadcast.
b It was from the moon.
c It wasn't silent.

4 Work in pairs. Compare opinions about 1–8. Use the key phrases in exercise 3.

In my opinion, the best channel is MTV.

I don't agree with you. I think VH1 is the best.

1 the best channel
2 the best show
3 the best presenter
4 the best advertisement
5 the worst presenter
6 the funniest character
7 the most boring program
8 the channel with the most advertisements

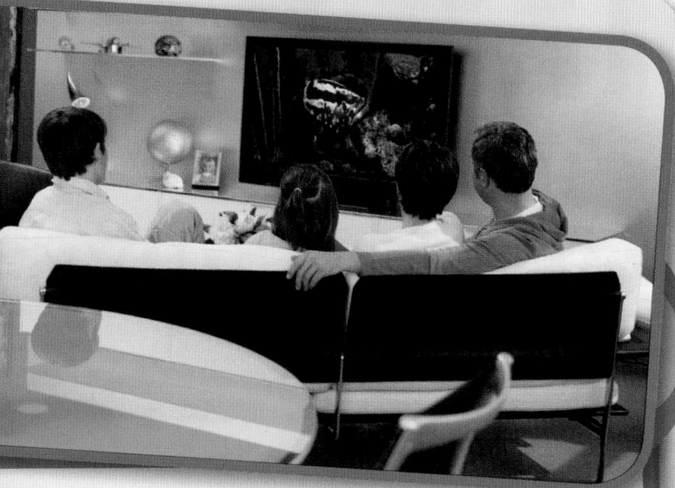

5 When was the first advertisement on TV and what was it for?
a 1901 (a bicycle) b 1981 (a toy)
c 1941 (a watch)

6 Which invention was popular with TV viewers in 1950?
a The first flat screen televisions.
b The first TV cameras.
c The first remote controls.

7 The first *Big Brother* program was on TV in 1999 in the Netherlands. Why was it popular?
a The participants weren't famous.
b There were cameras in the viewers' houses.
c The presenter wasn't famous.

8 Who was the star character in a famous action series with the same name? His favorite thing was a Swiss army knife.
a Homer Simpson b Dr. House
c MacGyver

Finished?
Write a paragraph giving your opinion about TV in your country.

was, were, there was, there were

5 Complete the sentences from the quiz. How do we make negative and question forms?

1 It ___ from the moon.
2 It ___ silent.
3 The participants ___ famous.
4 ___ it in 1979?
5 When ___ the first advertisement?
6 In the U.S. in 1985, there ___ 19 channels.
7 There ___ a historic TV broadcast in 1969.

More practice ⇨ Workbook page 9

6 Complete the dialogue with *was / wasn't* and *were / weren't*.

Dan There [1]___ a new show on TV yesterday.
Kim Really? What [2]___ it?
Dan It [3]___ a new reality show.
Kim [4]___ it the one on an island?
Dan No, it [5]___ that one. It [6]___ called *Stars*.
Kim Oh, yeah? [7]___ there any interesting participants on it?
Dan No, there [8]___, and the presenters [9]___ terrible. They [10]___ funny at all.
Kim Oh, dear! It's lucky I [11]___ at home, then! I [12]___ at the movies!

7 Complete the questions with the words in the box. Then ask and answer with a partner.

Were there	Who were	~~Was there~~
What was	How was	What were

Was there anything good on TV yesterday? What?

1 ___ the best TV program you watched last week? What was it about?
2 ___ your favorite TV programs when you were a child? Why?
3 ___ the characters on these programs?
4 ___ TV different in the past?
5 ___ other forms of entertainment before TV?

Was there anything good on TV yesterday?

Yes, there was a good episode of Glee. It was very funny.

8 ACTIVATE Work in pairs and write a quiz about TV in your country. Then swap with another pair and do their quiz. Use the key phrases.

READING ■ Reality TV

I can understand a text about reality TV.

1 1.07 **Look at the pictures and the title of the text. What do you think the text is about? Choose the correct answer. Then read, listen, and check your answer.**

a Reality shows that teenagers like best.
b How reality shows choose young participants.
c Using young people in reality shows.

2 **Read the text again and choose the correct answers.**

1 The early reality TV shows were ...
 a only for adults.
 b entertaining.
 c embarrassing for participants.
2 People take part in reality shows because ...
 a they are funny.
 b a lot of people watch them.
 c they receive money.
3 In *Kid Nation*, the TV company gave money to ...
 a the youngsters' parents.
 b all the young people.
 c the best participants.
4 *Kid Nation* shocked many people because ...
 a it was successful.
 b the channel made a lot of money.
 c the show used children to make money.
5 The writer thinks that the problem with reality TV is that ...
 a it is shocking, but successful.
 b it makes too much money.
 c the participants are children.

3 **BUILD YOUR VOCABULARY Write the past forms of the verbs in the box. Then read the text again and check. Which past forms are regular and which are irregular?**

~~live~~ ~~make~~ show choose leave love win try broadcast become attract solve receive follow do

lived – regular *made – irregular*

4 **Make a list of ten verbs and write the past forms. Check in the irregular verbs list in the Workbook. Then test your partner.**

What's the past of "take"? *Took.*

Pronunciation: Past tense *-ed* endings
⇨ Workbook page 90

5 **YOUR OPINIONS Ask and answer the questions.**

1 Do you think reality shows are cruel or embarrassing for the participants?
2 Do you think there should be a minimum age for participants in reality shows? Why / Why not?
3 Why do people like reality shows?
4 Which reality shows are popular in your country? Are they good?
5 Would you like to be in a reality show? Why / Why not?

HARD REALITY
Teenagers in reality shows

Reality shows use ordinary people instead of actors and this is nothing new. The first reality show, called *Candid Camera*, was in 1948 and it showed ordinary people in funny situations. In 1950, the reality show *Beat the Clock* became a huge success. Participants did amusing, but fun, tasks within a time limit. These early shows were entertaining, and participants and viewers loved them. But today's shows are different. Shows like *Big Brother* or *Survivor* are often cruel or embarrassing for the participants. So why do thousands of people want to take part in them? The answer is money. TV companies pay people to take part. Perhaps this is all right when the participants are adults, but it's different when they're children or teenagers.

1 **Complete the sentences from the text. Which words do we use to form the negative and question forms? Find more simple past sentences in the text.**

1 Cameras ___ them everywhere.
2 The show ___ big audiences.
3 The TV company ___ a second series.
4 ___ the young people ___ the experience?

More practice ⇨ Workbook page 9

In the reality show *Kid Nation*, forty young people between the ages of eight and fifteen lived together in an abandoned town for forty days. The young people tried to organize their lives without adults, and cameras followed them everywhere. The youngsters all received $5,000 for taking part in the show. In every episode, a participant who solved problems and made decisions won a prize of $20,000. The group chose this person. Did the young people enjoy the experience? It seems that some participants left before the end of the series because they didn't like it. They were lonely and unhappy.

The TV company didn't make a second series of *Kid Nation*. Many people were shocked and said that it was wrong to use children for fun and profit. Nevertheless, the show attracted big audiences and the channel that broadcast it made a lot of money. Perhaps that's the problem with reality TV shows now – the more they shock, the more successful they are.

2 **Complete the sentences with the correct form of the verbs in parentheses.**

1 Channel 2 ___ a reality show about cats. (broadcast)
2 He ___ the end of the program. (not see)
3 She ___ a million dollars on a TV show. (win)
4 They ___ the series on HBO. (not like)
5 I ___ a movie of my friends over my vacation. (make)

3 **Complete the text with the correct form of the verbs in the box.**

not be	put	~~be~~	have	record
not win	not play	eliminate	become	

Reality Cats

In one American reality show, the participants **were** cats. A TV company [1]___ ten cats in a small house and [2]___ them with cameras. Most of the cats were happy and they [3]___ bored. They [4]___ good food and a lot of toys.

Every day, the public [5]___ a cat for various reasons. One cat, for example, [6]___ with the toys. The last cat [7]___ a prize, but after the show the cats [8]___ famous.

4 **ACTIVATE** **Interview your partner about situations 1–6.**

(make) breakfast this morning? / What ... ?

Did you make breakfast this morning?

Yes, I did.

What did you make?

I made some toast.

1 (watch) TV last night? / What ... ?
2 (go) on vacation last year? / Where ... ?
3 (meet) a friend last weekend? / Who ... ?
4 (argue) with your parents yesterday? / Why ... ?
5 (play) video games last week? / Which ... ?
6 (buy) new clothes last month? / What ... ?

Finished?
Describe what happened on a TV program that you saw last week.

VOCABULARY AND LISTENING ■ On TV

I can understand and present news.

1 Complete the table with the words in the box and your own answers. Then ask and answer with a partner.

~~drama series~~ talent show reality show chat show medical drama ~~documentary~~ movie cartoon weather forecast sitcom quiz show game show sports program soap opera the news

Type of program	Your favorite program	When did you last watch it?
drama series documentary	CSI: NY	last night

What's your favorite drama series?

I like *CSI: NY*.

When did you last watch it?

I watched it last night.

2 1.08 Listen. What types of television program do you hear?

3 1.09 Look at pictures A–D. What do you think the news stories are about? Listen to the news and check.

STUDY STRATEGY ■ Listening for specific information

4 Read the questions in exercise 5 and underline important words for meaning.

5 1.09 Listen again and choose the correct answers.

1 Who was wearing protective glasses?
   a Robert Green b Billy Evans
   c President Obama
2 People ___ when it started snowing.
   a slept in their cars b were driving home
   c were making coffee
3 Were the police doing anything when the traffic stopped?
   a They were eating breakfast.
   b They were talking to people.
   c No, because weren't there.
4 What was the man doing in the park?
   a He was sitting under a tree.
   b He was looking for a friend.
   c He was walking to work.
5 The robber was ___ when Mrs. Banks stopped him.
   a lying on the ground
   b running to the door
   c shouting at the assistant

6 ACTIVATE Choose one of the photos A–D. Present the news item to your partner.

A lion escaped from a zoo yesterday. It disappeared into a forest. A man saw ...

LANGUAGE FOCUS ■ Past tenses

I can talk about what people were doing.

Past continuous

1 **Complete the sentences from exercise 5 on page 12 with the words in the box. Then choose the correct words in the rule.**

weren't	doing	were	was	Were

1 People ___ driving home.
2 The robber ___ running to the door.
3 ___ the police doing anything?
4 No, because they ___ there.
5 What was the man ___ in the park?

RULE

We use the past continuous when we talk about **short actions** / **actions in progress** in the past.

More practice ⇨ Workbook page 11

2 **Look at the picture. What were the people doing at 2 p.m. yesterday? Write sentences. Then ask and answer with a partner.**

Dad / talk on the phone
Dad wasn't talking on the phone. He was reading the newspaper.

1 Grandma / listen to music
2 Dad / watch a movie on TV
3 The dog / eat under the table
4 Gary and Ann / fight for the remote control
5 Mom / read newspaper
6 Grandpa and the cat / sleep

Was Dad talking on the phone at 2 p.m. yesterday?

No, he wasn't. He was reading the newspaper.

3 1.10 **Write questions using the past continuous. Then listen to part of a movie and answer the questions.**

1 Was / Dave (joke)?
2 Where / Jane (go)?
3 What / she (carry)?
4 How much money / she (carry) in it?
5 How many people / (work) in the gang?
6 Where / Pete (stand)?

Simple past and past continuous

4 **Match examples 1–3 with descriptions a–c. Which tenses do we use in each sentence?**

1 I was driving home when the traffic stopped.
2 The President was wearing protective glasses.
3 A man with a gun walked into the bank at 9:30.

a An action in progress in the past.
b A finished action in the past.
c A short, finished action and a longer, continuous action.

More practice ⇨ Workbook page 11

5 **Write sentences with *when* / *while* and the words below.**

Mom / sleep / I leave home
My mom was sleeping when I left home this morning.

1 friend / arrive / I do homework
2 the teacher / talk to us / bell ring
3 Dad turn off the TV / we / watch *House*
4 friends / play chess / we arrive
5 I / listen to music / brother / call

6 ACTIVATE **Work in pairs. Write a story about the family in the picture in exercise 2. Use the simple past and the past continuous tense and *when* / *while*. Tell your story to the rest of the class.**

Finished?

Imagine you looked at five different TV channels. What was happening on each one?

There was a sports program on ESPN.

Federer was winning the game.

SPEAKING ■ My news

I can talk about my news.

1 **Look at the picture. Vanessa is telling Marcus her news. Can you guess what it is about?**

2 1.11 **Listen to the dialogue. Why is Vanessa happy?**

Marcus	Hi, Vanessa. You look happy.
Vanessa	Oh, yes. I have some amazing news.
Marcus	Really? Tell me all about it.
Vanessa	Well, I sent a CD with my songs to the talent show on Channel 9 a month ago.
Marcus	Yes. What happened?
Vanessa	Well, I had an audition yesterday.
Marcus	You're kidding! How did it go?
Vanessa	It was really good. Five other people were auditioning, too.
Marcus	That's good news.
Vanessa	Yeah. What about you? What's your news?
Marcus	Oh, no news, really. So, maybe see you soon on TV?
Vanessa	Yes, maybe! See you around.
Marcus	Bye, Vanessa. Good luck.

3 **Complete the key phrases from the dialogue. Who says them? Then practice the dialogue with a partner.**

KEY PHRASES ○ Talking about news

You [1]___ happy / fed up / pleased.
I [2]___ some amazing / good / bad / terrible news.
Really?
Tell me [3]___ it.
What happened?
You're [4]___!
How did it [5]___?
That's good [6]___.
What's [7]___ news?

4 1.12 **Listen and choose the correct answers.**

1 a That's terrible! b Good luck. c That's great!
2 a Really? b Sorry to hear it. c Good for you!
3 a How did it go? b Tell me all about it. c That's good news.
4 a Tell me all about it. b We'll see. c What about you?
5 a You're kidding! b That's bad news. c What happened?

5 1.13 **Read and listen to the dialogues. Then practice mini-dialogues for situations 1–5 with a partner.**

Abby	Hi, Nick. How are things?
Nick	Fine, thanks. I have some good news. We won the basketball final.
Abby	That's great! Congratulations!

Luke	Hi, John. You don't look happy.
John	No, someone stole my car while I was shopping yesterday.
Luke	Oh, that's bad news! Sorry to hear it.

1 (pass) my music test
2 (win) a prize
3 (lose) $20
4 (break up) with my boyfriend / girlfriend
5 (record) a CD

6 **ACTIVATE** **Prepare a new dialogue with a partner. Use one of the situations in exercise 5 or your own ideas. Practice your dialogue. Then change roles.**

WRITING ■ A news article

I can write a news item.

1

Tunnel chaos

This was the dramatic scene last night on a train in the Channel Tunnel between France and England. More than five hundred passengers were stuck for hours when a train broke down.

The incident happened late yesterday afternoon. The train suddenly stopped while it was traveling through the tunnel.

At first, passengers waited calmly, but after several hours, the situation became very difficult. There was no food or water, and there weren't enough toilets on the train. Then the rescue services arrived, and they transferred people onto another train as soon as they could.

After sixteen hours, all the passengers were finally off the train. Later, one of them said, "People were sleeping on the floor and children were crying. It was terrible."

1 Read the model text and answer the questions.

1 Where can you find a text like this?
   a In a magazine. **b** In a movie guide.
   c In a newspaper.
2 Where and when did the incident happen?
3 What were the conditions on the train?
4 What did the rescue services do?
5 How did the passengers react?

2 Study the key phrases. Put them in the order of the text. Then read the model text again and check.

KEY PHRASES ○ Writing a news item

a The incident happened (late yesterday afternoon). ___
b People were (sleeping ...) and ... ___
c There was no ... and there weren't ... ___
d This was the dramatic scene ... ___
e Later, one of them said, ... ___

Language point: Time connectors

3 Find these words in the model text. When do we use them? Choose the correct answers in sentences 1–6.

when while as soon as later at first after then finally

1 At first, people were calm, but **later / after** they became angry.
2 The rescue services arrived at the scene **as soon as / while** they could.
3 The passengers **finally / then** arrived in London.
4 The train stopped, and **then / at first** the lights went out.
5 **When / While** the train stopped, people weren't worried.
6 **After / Then** the incident, the train company apologized to the passengers.

4 ACTIVATE Follow the steps in the writing guide.

○ WRITING GUIDE

A TASK

Write a news item about the incident in picture B or C on page 12, or use your own idea.

B THINK AND PLAN

1 Where, when, and why did the incident happen?
2 What caused the incident?
3 What were conditions like?
4 How did people react? What were people doing?
5 What happened in the end?
6 What did people say?

C WRITE

Paragraph 1: Introduction
This was the dramatic scene ...
Paragraph 2: The incident
The incident began ...
Paragraph 3: Conditions
At first, ...
Paragraph 4: Conclusion and reaction
After ... hours, ...

D CHECK

- time connectors
- simple past and past continuous

REVIEW Unit 1

Vocabulary

1 Complete the dialogue with the words in the box.

participants remote control advertisements show episode program channels

Ken Can I change [1]___? I hate watching [2]___.
Kate But there's a good [3]___ on in a few minutes.
Ken What is it?
Kate A reality [4]___ called *The Farm*. The [5]___ are famous people.
Ken But there's the next [6]___ of my favorite series on Channel 6.
Kate Oh, all right. Here's the [7]___!

2 Reorder the letters to make TV programs.

1 cmaordunyet ___
2 naltet hswo ___
3 otaorcn ___
4 mdara risees ___
5 het wesn ___
6 smitoc ___
7 eomiv ___
8 psrost gamropr ___

Language focus

3 Complete the sentences using the simple past form of the verbs in parentheses.

1 There ___ (be) a talent show on TV last night.
2 In the 1980s, TV programs ___ (not be) in black and white.
3 We ___ (not watch) TV yesterday.
4 I ___ (meet) my friends after school.
5 My mother ___ (take) part in a reality show.
6 He ___ (not complain) when I ___ (change) channels.

4 Write questions and short answers for the sentences in exercise 3.

Was there a talent show on TV last night?
Yes, there was.

5 Complete the sentences using the simple past or past continuous form of the verbs in parentheses.

1 Rob ___ (watch) the news when I ___ (arrive).
2 Jo ___ (not wear) her hat when I ___ (meet) her.
3 I ___ (not go) to school because I was sick.
4 ___ (you see) the sports program last night?
5 We ___ (break) the TV when we ___ (argue).
6 My mom ___ (change) the channel while I ___ (watch) a good movie.

Communication

6 Choose the correct answers.

1 What happened?
a It was great! b I won a prize. c No, I didn't.
2 You look pleased.
a I'm fed up. b It's fantastic. c I have some good news.
3 I think she's the best presenter on TV.
a He's awful! b I agree with you. c Not really.
4 What's your news?
a Nothing much. b That's good. c Really?
5 Was there anything good on TV yesterday?
a It wasn't. b Yes, it was. c Yes, there was.
6 I have some bad news.
a That's good news. b What happened? c I'm not sure about that.

Listening

7 1.14 **Listen to four people talking about television. Match speakers 1–4 with sentences a–e. There is one sentence that you do not need.**

Speaker 1 ___ Speaker 3 ___
Speaker 2 ___ Speaker 4 ___

a I watched an episode of a drama series last night.
b I want to take part in a reality show.
c Young people today watch too much TV.
d I didn't see a friend on a talent show.
e TV is better today because there are more channels.

PROJECT A TV program

1 1.15 **Read the scripts of three TV programs and match them with the types of program in the box. Then listen to the complete programs.**

soap opera weather forecast documentary
chat show comedy sports news movie
reality show drama quiz show cooking show

A

Presenter	Good evening and welcome to *Cheap Cook*! Our celebrity chef tonight is Billy Brunch from The Eggy House in Chicago. What are you cooking for us, Billy?
Billy	Hello. Well, at The Eggy House we use a lot of eggs, so tonight I'm doing a classic egg recipe. It's called Eggy Bread. My grandma gave me this recipe. It was her favorite winter meal.
Presenter	So, it's perfect for tonight!
Billy	That's right, and it's one of the cheapest meals you can make.
Presenter	Really? Now, what do you ... ?

B

Presenter	Welcome to *Showing Off*. I'm Sharon Stewart and my guest tonight is soccer player Ryan Looney.
Ryan	Good evening.
Presenter	Ryan, you are playing for Real Madrid this year. Why did you leave Porto when you were playing so well there?
Ryan	It was time to move. I was playing well, but I wasn't earning a lot of money. Now I am.
Presenter	Oh, so you moved because ....

C

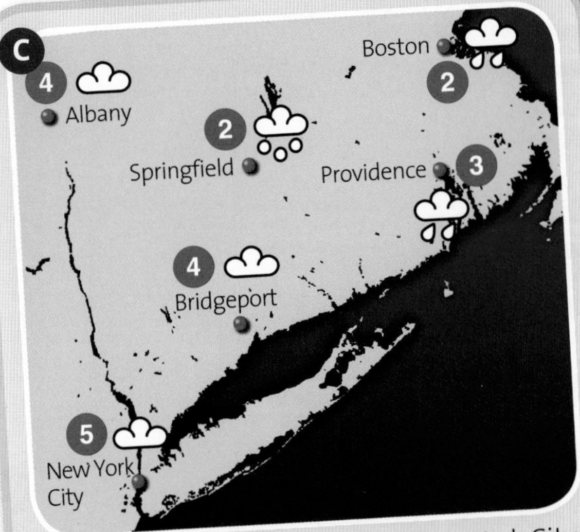

Good evening. It's quite cold in New York City at the moment. Temperatures are between 2°C and 7°C in the daytime, and colder than that at night. In Boston last night, temperatures were around 2°C. That's colder than usual for the season. Right now, it is snowing in ... .

2 Work in groups. Write the script for a TV program. Follow the steps in the project checklist.

PROJECT CHECKLIST

1. Choose one of the program types in exercise 1 or another type of program.
2. Choose a name for your program and decide on your roles.
3. Write a script for your program. Include notes on where people are, what they are doing, and any sound effects.
4. Practice your TV program in pairs or in groups.

3 Present your TV program to the rest of the class. Which TV programs are the best?

2 Disposable world

Start thinking

1 Who are consumers?
2 How can people create less trash?
3 How can plastic bags be a problem?

Aims

Communication: I can ...

- talk about quantities of things people use.
- understand a text about a "no impact" family.
- talk about places, people, and things using relative pronouns.
- understand a program about pollution and the environment.
- talk about eating habits.
- offer and ask for help.
- write about an environmental problem.

Vocabulary

- Household goods
- Pollution and the environment

Language focus

- *much, many, a lot of, some, any*
- Relative pronouns
- *too, too much, many, enough, not enough*

Reach Out Options

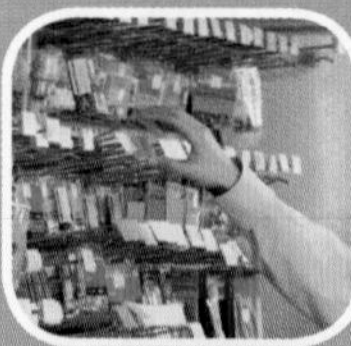

Extra listening and speaking
Explaining what you want to buy
Page 89

Curriculum extra
Geography: Sustainable development
Page 97

Culture
Clean Up the World
Page 105

Vocabulary bank
Compound nouns; Waste
Page 113

VOCABULARY AND LANGUAGE FOCUS
Household goods

I can talk about quantities of things people use.

1 1.20 Match the words in the boxes with pictures 1–10. Then listen and check your answers.

bottle roll carton ~~can~~ tube box jar package bag bar

juice toothpaste ~~soda~~ toilet paper coffee chocolate laundry detergent potato chips apples shampoo

1 a can of soda

2 Work in pairs. Think of more containers and contents.

a cup of coffee

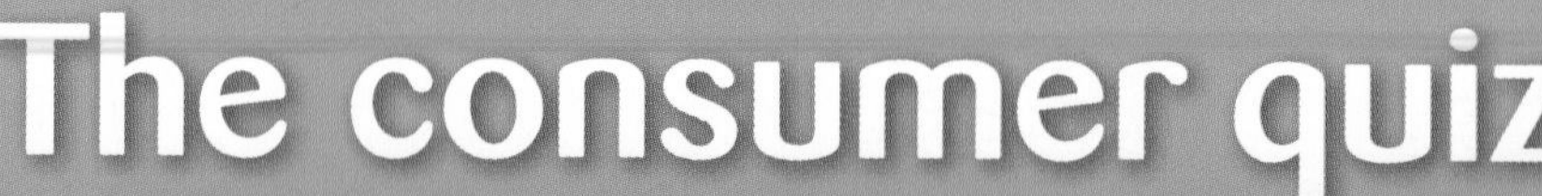

The consumer quiz

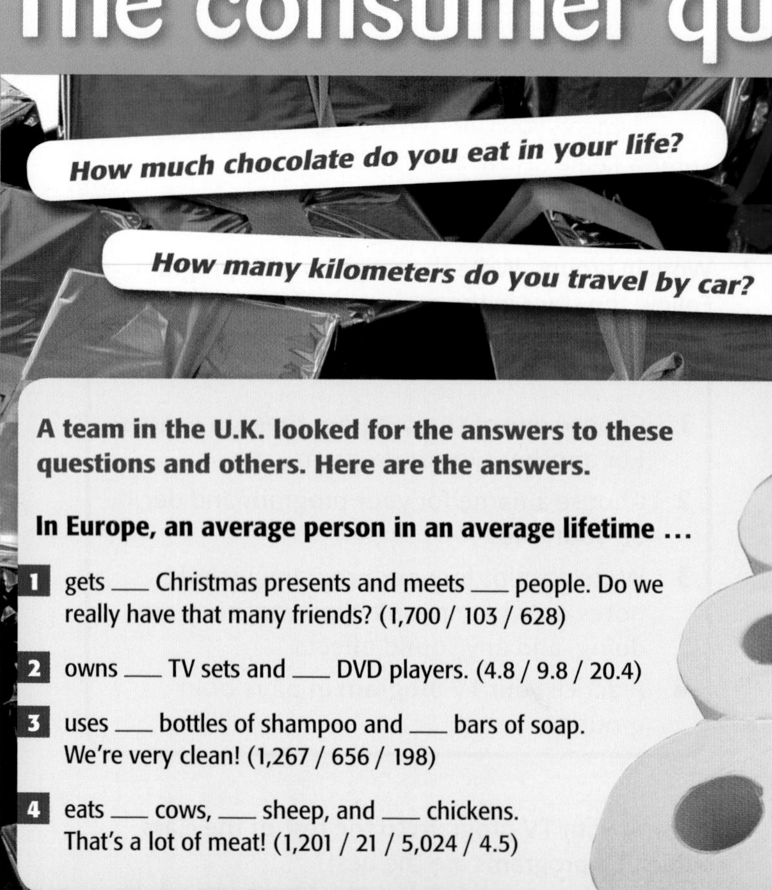

How much chocolate do you eat in your life?

How many kilometers do you travel by car?

A team in the U.K. looked for the answers to these questions and others. Here are the answers.

In Europe, an average person in an average lifetime ...

1 gets ___ Christmas presents and meets ___ people. Do we really have that many friends? (1,700 / 103 / 628)

2 owns ___ TV sets and ___ DVD players. (4.8 / 9.8 / 20.4)

3 uses ___ bottles of shampoo and ___ bars of soap. We're very clean! (1,267 / 656 / 198)

4 eats ___ cows, ___ sheep, and ___ chickens. That's a lot of meat! (1,201 / 21 / 5,024 / 4.5)

3 1.21 **Study the key phrases and write the numbers. Listen and say the numbers.**

KEY PHRASES Saying numbers

1 One point three.
2 One hundred one.
3 Fourteen thousand, five hundred forty.
4 Thirty two thousand, nine hundred eight.
5 One hundred twenty-five thousand.
6 Two million.

4 1.22 **Do *The consumer quiz*. Guess the answers. There is one answer that you do not need. Compare your answers to the quiz with a partner. Then listen and check.**

5 eats ___ bars of chocolate and ___ cans of beans, if the person is British. That's a lot of chocolate and beans! (72 / 854 / 10,354)

6 uses ___ tons of fuel in ___ different cars. That's bad news for the planet! (8 / 120,000 / 64)

7 walks more than ___ kilometers and drives more than ___ kilometers. That's from here to the moon and back! (720,000 / 493 / 24,000)

8 uses ___ tubes of toothpaste and ___ rolls of toilet paper. That's over 185 kilometers of paper! (276 / 4,239 / 109)

9 drinks ___ cups of tea or coffee, ___ glasses of milk, and ___ cans of soda. Not very healthy! (74,802 / 49,717 / 598,201 / 38,320)

much, many, a lot of, some, any

5 **Read the sentences. Are the nouns countable or uncountable? Complete the table with the words in blue.**

1 How much chocolate do you eat?
2 How many kilometers do you walk?
3 There aren't many books here.
4 There isn't much toothpaste.
5 Do you use much fuel?
6 I buy a lot of bread, but I don't buy many potatoes or much pasta.
7 I have some apples and some milk.
8 There aren't any oranges and there isn't any sugar.

Uncountable nouns	Countable nouns
How much not much 2 ___ 3 ___ a little 4 ___ not any	How many 1 ___ many a lot of a few / one or two some 5 ___

More practice ⇨ Workbook page 17

6 **Choose the correct words.**

1 Do you eat **much** / **many** cheese?
2 How **many** / **any** kilometers do you travel every month?
3 I have **any** / **some** chocolate in my bag.
4 How **much** / **many** water do you drink each day?
5 There isn't **some** / **any** shampoo.
6 Is there **many** / **any** tea left?

7 **ACTIVATE Work in pairs. Ask and answer 1–6 with your own ideas. Use the phrases in the table in exercise 5 and numbers. Guess if you do not know the exact answer.**

eat / eggs / each week

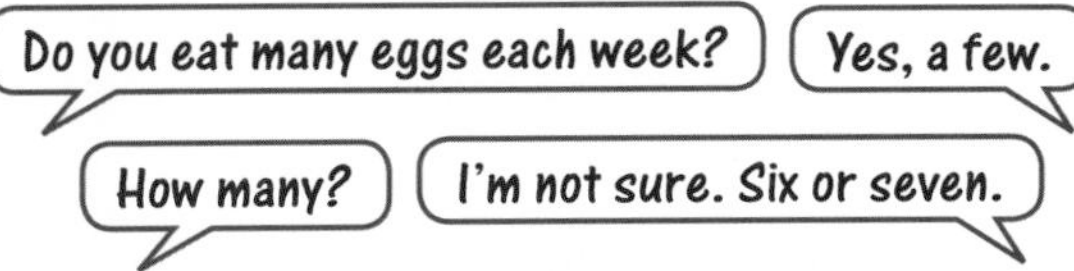

1 eat / pasta / each week
2 walk / kilometers / every month
3 be / books / the school library
4 use / toothpaste / each year
5 drink / milk / every week
6 say / words / every day

Finished?
Write about the things that you use, eat, and drink in a week.
I drink four cans of soda in a week.

READING ■ The "no impact" family

I can understand a text about a "no impact" family.

STUDY STRATEGY ○ Predicting

1 Look at the pictures and the title of the text. Predict which of the sentences 1–6 are *true* or *false*. Then read the text and check your answers.

The "no impact" family ...

1 lives in a big city.
2 uses a lot of electricity.
3 makes its own soap.
4 is interested in the environment.
5 prefers shopping at big supermarkets.
6 prefers not to use plastic bags and packages.

2 1.23 Complete the text with sentences a–e. There is one sentence that you do not need. Then listen and check your answers.

a Colin always carries a glass jar.
b They don't buy these things now.
c They travel everywhere by bicycle.
d Colin drinks a lot of coffee.
e He says that it's interesting to try these things.

3 BUILD YOUR VOCABULARY Read the information and complete the examples. Then find four more compound nouns in the text.

Some compound nouns are combinations of word + noun. The first word describes the second noun.

Examples

shopping bag – a bag which is for [1]___
bedroom – a room which has a [2]___
washing machine – a machine which [3]___ clothes

4 Complete the sentences with the words in the box.

strawberry shopping paper
chicken Christmas laundry

1 I'd like some ___ ice cream, please.
2 What can I buy Sam for a ___ present?
3 You can buy a camera at the ___ mall.
4 There isn't any ___ detergent left.
5 You can wipe it with ___ towel.
6 Is that a ___ sandwich?

5 YOUR OPINIONS Ask and answer the questions.

1 What do you think about the family's experiment?
2 What do you think the family finds most difficult to live without? Why?
3 Are there any things in your house that you do not need?
4 Do you and your family have a big impact on the environment?
5 What can you do to reduce your impact?

Pronunciation: Word stress in compound nouns
⇨ Workbook page 90

THE "NO IMPACT" FAMIL

Can you imagine life with no TV? What about no toilet paper?

In the Beavan family's New York apartment, there isn't a TV, a washing machine, a dishwasher, or a fridge, and they're only using one electric light bulb. In the bathroom, there aren't any shampoo bottles, rolls of toilet paper, or tubes of toothpaste. [1]___ They make them or use alternatives.

Some people think that they're crazy, but Colin Beavan explains that it's just an experiment. [2]___ The Beavans are living like this for a year because they want to reduce their impact on the environment. At the end of the year, they'll decide what they really need and what they can live without.

They're trying to create less trash and use less electricity and fuel. The family doesn't travel by car or fly. [3]___ They buy second-hand things for the apartment and they buy food at a market, where they can avoid plastic bags, packages, and boxes. They carry the food home in a basket, not a plastic shopping bag. They don't buy any food which comes from more than 400 kilometers away.

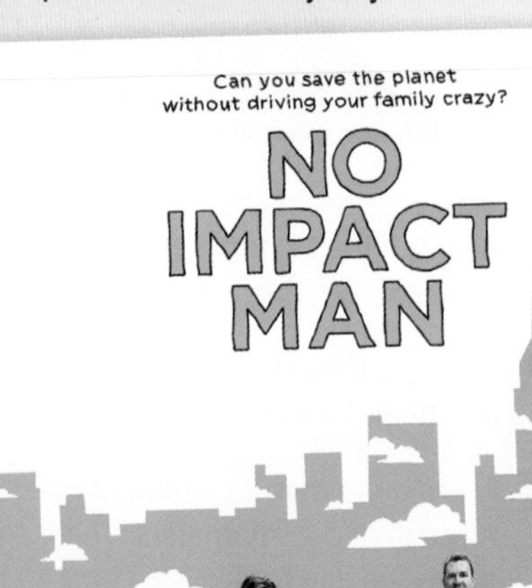

Can you save the planet without driving your family crazy?
NO IMPACT MAN
LOS ANGELES
SUNDANCE
SILVERDOCS

LANGUAGE FOCUS ■ Relative pronouns

I can talk about places, people, and things using relative pronouns.

2

1 Complete the sentences from the text. Then complete the rules with *places*, *people*, and *things*.

1 People ___ read his blog or book will think about how much they use.

2 In the places ___ Colin has coffee, they give it to him in his jar.

3 They don't buy food ___ comes from more than 400 kilometers away.

RULES

1 We use *who* when we talk about ___.

2 We use *where* when we talk about ___.

3 We use *which* when we talk about ___.

More practice ⇨ Workbook page 17

The Beavans also avoid takeout food which wastes a lot of containers. [4]___ In the places where Colin has coffee, they give it to him in his jar instead of a disposable plastic cup. They make their own yogurt, so they don't throw a lot of plastic containers away.

Colin says that the experiment is interesting, but it isn't always easy. He isn't trying to change other people's lifestyle, but he hopes that people who read his blog or book will think about how much they use and waste.

2 Complete the text with *who*, *where*, and *which*.

Think globally – buy locally!

People who want to protect the environment are usually careful about the origin of their food. Food [1]___ comes from local producers is OK, but the countries [2]___ farmers grow exotic fruits are often thousands of kilometers from our stores. A good example is kiwi fruit [3]___ comes by plane from New Zealand. The boxes of fruit arrive at our airports [4]___ trucks are waiting to transport them to supermarkets. The supermarkets [5]___ sell this product are often out of town, so people [6]___ buy kiwi fruit must drive there. All in all, that's a lot of boxes and fuel – a lot of waste.

3 Complete the sentences with your own ideas. Use *who*, *where*, or *which*. Compare with a partner.

A café is a place **where you can eat snacks**.

1 A farmer's market is a place ___.

2 Oranges and lemons are fruit ___.

3 A journalist is a person ___.

4 Work is something ___.

5 My friend is someone ___.

6 A whale is a mammal ___.

4 ACTIVATE Write six sentences with *who*, *where*, and *which*. Then play a guessing game with a partner.

This is	a drink a place something a person a program a café a club	who where which	I admire. I really like. makes me happy. makes me angry. I can meet friends. I can relax. I never buy. I have fun. I can do martial arts.

This is a place where I can relax.

Is it your bedroom?

No, the beach is a place where I can relax.

Finished?

Write four definitions using *who*, *where*, and *which*, and your own ideas.

Hot chocolate is a drink which I really like.

VOCABULARY AND LISTENING ■ Pollution and the environment

I can understand a program about pollution and the environment.

1 1.24 **Check the meaning of the words in blue. Choose the correct words. Then listen and check.**

A plastic problem

People use a lot of plastic bags and they often [1]throw away / bury the bags afterwards. They don't often [2]pollute / reuse or [3]waste / recycle them. When we [4]destroy / reuse plastic, we pollute the land or air. It isn't a good idea to [5]burn / poison plastic because it [6]poisons / saves the atmosphere. The alternative is to [7]bury / pollute it, but some plastic doesn't decompose for over a thousand years.

2 Work in pairs. Ask and answer the questions.

1 Do you throw away or reuse plastic bags?
2 What do you and your school do with trash?
3 How can you reduce waste in your home?
4 What happens to trash in your area?
5 What things are harmful to the environment in your area?

3 1.25 **Read the information about Rebecca Hosking. Order sentences a–d, then listen and check.**

a Rebecca spoke to people in her town.
b Rebecca was filming a wildlife documentary.
c People use cloth bags in Rebecca's town now.
d Rebecca saw that animals were dying.

4 1.25 **Listen again and write *true* or *false*. Correct the false sentences.**

1 The speaker is Rebecca Hosking.
2 She was shocked because plastic waste was killing the marine animals in her hometown.
3 Most people don't know where their plastic waste goes.
4 Sea birds think the plastic is food and eat it.
5 A few stores in Rebecca's town still give people plastic bags.
6 The program informs us about the dangers of plastic.

5 1.26 **Listen to a reporter in Rebecca's town. What was different a year later? Check the things she mentions.**

styrofoam cups   cardboard boxes
plastic shopping bags   waste food
bottle tops   laundry detergent
used cooking oil   paper bags   glass bottles
old newspapers   plastic sandwich boxes

6 ACTIVATE **Work in groups. Look at the list of waste products in exercise 5. Decide on the three things which pollute the environment the most. Then answer the questions.**

1 Which are the most dangerous to destroy?
2 How can you get rid of them?
3 What can you use instead of these things?

Battle of the bags

Rebecca Hosking is a professional camerawoman who lives near the coast in the south of England. When she was filming in the Pacific and she saw how plastic was affecting marine life, she decided to do something in her hometown.

LANGUAGE FOCUS ■ *too, too much, too many, enough, not enough*

I can talk about eating habits.

1 Study these sentences from the listening on page 22. Then complete the rules with *adjectives*, *countable nouns*, and *uncountable nouns*.

1 There's too much plastic.
2 There are too many plastic bags.
3 The council was too busy.

RULES

We use *too much* with [1]___, *too many* with [2]___, and *too* with [3]___.

More practice ⇨ Workbook page 19

2 Complete the sentences with *too*, *too much*, or *too many*.

1 This yogurt is ___ old.
2 We waste ___ food.
3 People throw away ___ bottles.
4 I drink ___ coffee.
5 There are ___ sandwiches for two people.
6 My mom thinks that I'm ___ greedy!
7 She says that I eat ___ potato chips and I drink ___ orange juice.

3 Study these sentences from the listening on page 22. Then complete the rules with *before* or *after*.

The problem was **serious** enough. (adjective)
We don't **recycle** enough. (verb)
There are enough **people** interested in a problem. (noun)

RULES

We use *enough*:
[1]___ adjectives,
[2]___ verbs,
[3]___ nouns.

More practice ⇨ Workbook page 19

4 1.27 **Order the words to make questions. Then listen to a conversation and answer the questions.**

1 we / sandwiches / enough / do / have
2 big / this pizza / enough / is
3 there / enough / are / apples
4 enough / this soup / hot / is
5 enough / this coffee / strong / is

5 Look at the shopping list and the shopping basket. Write sentences with *too much*, *too many*, *enough*, and *not enough*.

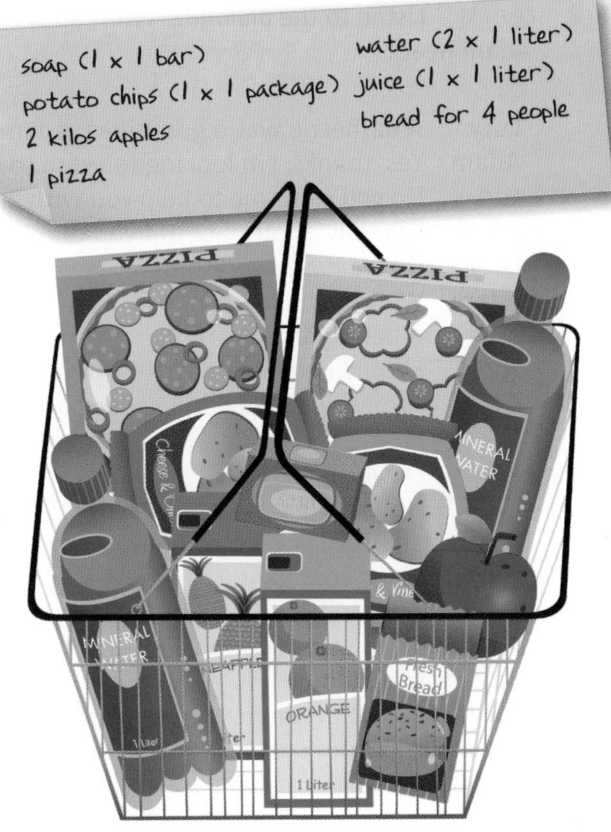

We have enough soap.
We have too many packages of potato chips.

6 ACTIVATE Find out about your partner's eating habits. Use 1–8 and your own ideas. Then tell the class about your partner's eating habits.

1 many potato chips
2 How much fruit
3 How much candy
4 too much sugar
5 too many sodas
6 enough vegetables
7 much coffee
8 enough milk

Do you eat many potato chips?
Yes, I eat too many.
How much fruit do you eat?
I don't eat enough. I don't like it.

My partner eats too many potato chips.
He / She doesn't eat enough fruit.

Finished?
Write sentences about problems in your town with *too*, *too much*, *too many*, *enough*, and *not enough*.
There aren't enough shopping malls.

SPEAKING ■ Offering and asking for help

I can offer and ask for help.

1 **Look at the picture. What are Lucy and Adam preparing?**

2 1.28 **Listen to the dialogue. What does Adam need?**

Lucy	A barbecue was a great idea, Adam.
Adam	Yes, thanks. I'm looking forward to it.
Lucy	Do you want me to help you with anything?
Adam	I'd really appreciate it if you don't mind.
Lucy	Do we have everything?
Adam	Well, we have enough food, but there isn't much to drink.
Lucy	Should I get a few cartons of juice or something? There's a supermarket near here.
Adam	Do you mind?
Lucy	No, that's fine.
Adam	Thanks, Lucy. Do you have enough money?
Lucy	Yes. If you want, I can get a bag of ice, too. We don't have any.
Adam	Good idea! Oh, and we need bags for the trash. Could you get some?
Lucy	OK, no problem. I'll see what they have.

3 1.29 **Cover the dialogue and complete the key phrases. Which phrases are for offering help and which are for asking for help? Listen and check. Then practice the dialogue with a partner.**

KEY PHRASES ○ Offering and asking for help

Do you want me to [1]___?
I'd really appreciate it if you don't mind.
Should I [2]___?
Do you mind?
If you want, I can [3]___.
Could you [4]___?
OK, no problem. I'll [5]___.

4 1.30 **Listen and repeat the sentences. Practice linking the words.**

1 A bag of ice.
2 A box of matches.
3 A bottle of soda.
4 A lot of bananas and apples.
5 We need a carton of juice.

5 **Study the key phrases again. Then complete the sentences with your own ideas.**

1 Your room is very dirty. Should I ___?
2 This homework is too difficult.
OK, no problem. I'll ___.
3 I don't want to go alone.
Should I ___?
4 You're very noisy. Could you ___?
5 There isn't any sugar left. Do you want me to ___?
6 We need to call Tom. Should I ___?

6 **ACTIVATE Prepare a new dialogue with a partner. Use the shopping lists or your own ideas. Practice your dialogue. Then change roles.**

Camping trip – shopping list
water ✔
sleeping bags ✘
map ✘
box of matches ✘
flashlight ✔

Boat trip – shopping list
sunscreen ✔
snack (fruit, sandwiches?) ✘
water ✘
life jackets ✔
sun hat ✘

WRITING ■ An environmental problem

I can write about an environmental problem.

2

1 **Read the model text and choose the correct answers.**

1 Why did the author write this e-mail?
   a To ask for an explanation. b To complain. c To offer help.

2 Who did he write the e-mail to?
   a a friend b a local newspaper c a tourist

3 Which word in the text expresses certainty?
   a perhaps b definitely c possibly

4 Which paragraph gives causes and solutions?
   a paragraph 1 b paragraph 3 c paragraph 2

2 **Study the key phrases. Which phrases introduce new paragraphs? Complete the phrases with your own ideas.**

KEY PHRASES ○ Writing an e-mail

I'm writing because ... .
This picture shows ... .
I think there are possibly (two) reasons for this.
Firstly / Secondly, ...
We must do something about ... .

Clean our beach!

Dear Sir / Madam,

I'm writing because I was at the beach with some friends last weekend and the amount of trash which we found there was unbelievable. This picture shows the bottles, cans, and other trash which we found.

I think there are possibly two reasons for this. Firstly, people aren't responsible enough and they throw their trash away anywhere. Perhaps we need a few signs and people who patrol the beach. Also, there aren't enough trash cans on or near the beach, so I think we need more. Secondly, nobody cleans the beach. I think this is terrible in a tourist town. We need people to clean the beach and empty the trash cans every day.

3 We must definitely do something about this situation. Maybe there isn't much trash in other places. I don't know, but we must do something here if we want a cleaner, more attractive beach.

Jon Adams

Language point: *so* and *because*

3 **Complete the examples from the text. Then match 1–5 with a–e. Use *so* or *because*.**

I'm writing ___.
There aren't enough trash cans, ___.

1 I went to the supermarket, ...
2 Cars pollute the environment, ...
3 There isn't much water, ...
4 I can't buy a present, ...
5 I threw away the letter, ...

a bicycles are better.
b I didn't want to read it.
c I don't have any money.
d we needed some shampoo.
e please don't drink too much.

4 **ACTIVATE Follow the steps in the writing guide.**

○ WRITING GUIDE

A TASK

Imagine that you took a picture of a traffic jam. Write an e-mail to a newspaper about the traffic problem in a city that you know.

B THINK AND PLAN

Can you think of any causes and solutions for the problems 1–3?

1 There's too much traffic.
2 There aren't enough buses.
3 Not many people use bikes.

C WRITE

Paragraph 1: Describe the situation
I'm writing because I was ... .
Paragraph 2: Causes and solutions
I think there are ... reasons for this.
Paragraph 3: Conclusion
We must do something about this situation.

D CHECK

- *so* and *because*
- *too, too much, too many, enough, not enough*
- *possibly, perhaps, maybe, definitely*

Vocabulary

1 Complete the phrases with the words in the box.

a cup a bar a roll a can a carton a package a bottle a tube

1 ___ of water
2 ___ of toilet paper
3 ___ of toothpaste
4 ___ of chocolate
5 ___ of tuna
6 ___ of coffee
7 ___ of potato chips
8 ___ of juice

2 Complete the sentences with the verbs in the box.

pollute recycle burn poisons waste bury save throw away

1 We shouldn't ___ bottles. It's better to ___ them.
2 You can ___ energy by using public transportation.
3 Nuclear power stations don't ___ the air, but they create dangerous waste.
4 Waste plastic ___ marine animals.
5 When you ___ plastic, dangerous gases go into the atmosphere.
6 If you ___ plastic, it will stay in the ground for 1,000 years.
7 You ___ energy when you leave the window open in winter.

Language focus

3 Choose the correct words.

1 Does your family recycle **much** / **many** glass bottles?
2 Do you eat **too much** / **too many** chocolate?
3 How **much** / **many** hours do you study every day?
4 We throw away **a lot of** / **many** trash.
5 I don't have **any** / **some** toothpaste left.
6 There isn't **enough** / **many** fuel to heat the house.
7 How **much** / **many** kilometers do you walk each day?
8 I ate **too much** / **too many** candy and now I feel sick.
9 He isn't **fast enough** / **too fast** to win the race.
10 Do we protect animals **too** / **enough**?

4 Match the two parts of the sentences. Then complete the sentences with *who*, *which*, and *where*.

1 The farmers
2 I buy apples
3 That's the store
4 That's the club
5 He's the person
6 I don't like food

a my brother works.
b has a lot of packaging.
c come from local farmers.
d discovered Australia.
e produce milk work hard.
f we go on Saturday nights.

Communication

5 Complete the dialogue with the phrases in the box.

a lot If you want some How much that's fine

Greg [1]___ food is there?
Jo There are [2]___ of sandwiches and a package of potato chips.
Greg What about cake? [3]___, I can make a chocolate cake.
Jo Do you mind?
Greg No, [4]___. I have chocolate and I can buy [5]___ eggs.

Listening

6 1.31 **Listen to a conversation about a "no impact" lifestyle. Write *true* or *false*.**

1 The woman is interviewing Colin Beavan about his "no impact" lifestyle.
2 Joe started the "no impact" lifestyle a month ago.
3 Joe doesn't buy any fruit or vegetables which come from faraway countries.
4 Joe gets a lot of fruit and vegetables from supermarkets.
5 Joe doesn't throw away a lot of trash.
6 Joe rides his bike a lot.

Listening

1 Look at the pictures and answer the questions.

1. What type of event is this?
2. What happens there?
3. Which picture shows the end of the event?
4. Who do you think cleans up after the event?
5. How could the organizers change this?

2 1.32 **Listen to a conversation. Who went to Lollapalooza last year? What didn't this person like?**

3 1.32 **Listen again and complete the sentences.**

1. ___ couldn't buy a ticket.
2. ___ is selling her ticket to ___.
3. Liza doesn't need a ticket because she's a ___.
4. ___ is going to call the hostel.
5. ___ is buying the food.
6. ___ is getting the bus tickets.
7. They should each take an ___.
8. They're leaving next ___.

Speaking

4 Work in groups of three and prepare a conversation. Imagine you are going to Lollapalooza. One of you went there last year and is organizing the trip. Answer the questions.

1. What was it like last year?
2. How are you getting there?
3. How long are you staying?
4. Where are you staying?
5. What is each person taking? Think about food, drinks, umbrellas, etc.

5 Have a conversation. Use your ideas in exercise 4 and the chart below to help you. One of you is A, one of you is B and one of you is C. Change roles.

- **A** Tell B and C your plans.
- **B** *That sounds ... !*
- **A** Invite B and C.
- **B** Accept.
- **C** Ask where people stay.
- **A** Reply.
- **C** Offer to help.
- **A** Ask C to find you a place to stay.
- **C** Reply.
- **B** Offer to find transportation.
- **A** Reply.

Writing

6 Write a comment on the festival website. Describe your festival experience. Mention one thing about the festival organization that you didn't like and suggest a way of improving this for next year. Begin like this:

I went to ... in ... . It was fantastic and the music was... . The only problem was ... .

Life online

Start thinking

1 What search engines do you know?
2 Do you know any Internet addicts?
3 Who are cybercriminals?

Aims

Communication: I can ...

- talk about my experiences.
- understand a text about Internet addiction.
- talk about Internet use.
- talk about cybercrime.
- ask and answer about experiences.
- apologize for something and explain how it happened.
- write an opinion comment on a website.

Vocabulary

- The Internet
- Cybercrime

Language focus

- Present perfect: affirmative and negative
- Present perfect: regular and irregular verbs
- Present perfect: questions

Reach Out Options

Extra listening and speaking

Talking about websites

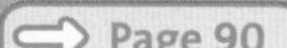

Page 90

Curriculum extra

Technology:
The Internet – wikis

Page 98

Culture

Social networks around the world

Page 106

Vocabulary bank

Verb and noun collocations; Personal details

Page 114

VOCABULARY AND LANGUAGE FOCUS
The Internet

I can talk about my experiences.

1 1.37 Complete the table with words or phrases from the *Are you well-connected?* questionnaire. Then listen and check.

Nouns	Verbs
e-mail	e-mail
instant messaging (IM)	message people
download	[1]___
file sharing	[2]___ files
[3]___ board	post a message
[4]___	blog
personal webpage	[5]___ a personal webpage
[6]___ room	chat
online game	[7]___ games online
[8]___ engine	search
webcam	[9]___ a webcam
e-mail [10]___	send an e-mail attachment

Are you well-connected

1 I've e-mailed or messaged people in another country.
2 I've downloaded music or movies from the Internet.
3 I've shared music or movie files with people on the Internet.
4 I've joined a social networking site like Facebook or Orkut.
5 I've posted a message on a message board.
6 I've created a blog or a personal webpage.
7 I've logged onto a chat room recently.
8 I've posted a video or pictures of myself on a website.
9 I've played games with people online.
10 I've used a search engine to help me research answers to my homework.
11 I've used a webcam to have a video chat session with a friend.
12 I've sent an e-mail attachment.

Key

8 or more *Yes* answers
You're super-connected. Are you living online? Remember there's a real world, too!

3 to 7 *Yes* answers
You know your way around the Internet, but you still make time to disconnect.

1 or 2 *Yes* answers
You've decided to disconnect or live in the real world. It isn't a bad place, is it?

2 Do the questionnaire. Answer *yes* or *no*. Then check the key. Compare your answers with a partner.

3 Work in pairs. Ask and answer questions using the nouns and verbs in exercise 1.

Do you e-mail friends?

Yes, sometimes, but I prefer instant messaging.

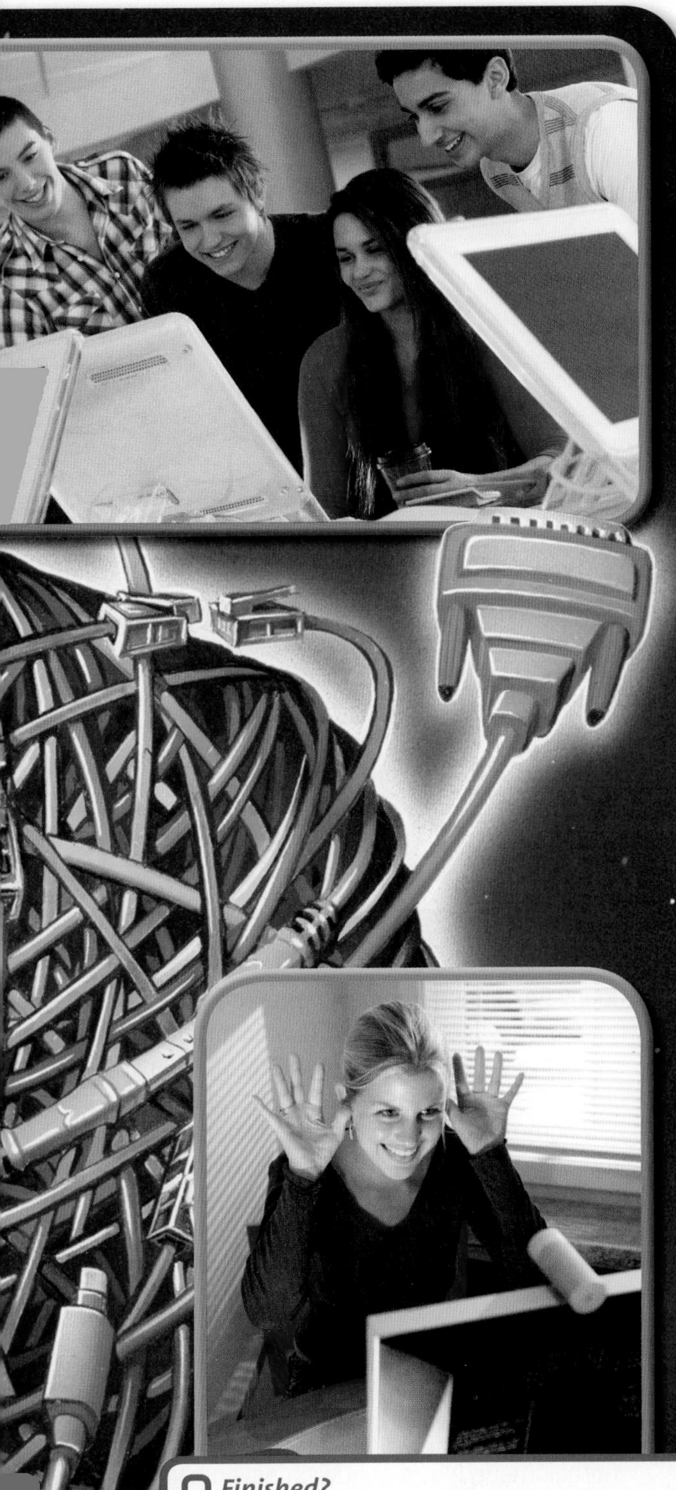

Present perfect: affirmative and negative

4 Study the examples. What are the long forms of *'ve*, *'s*, *hasn't*, and *haven't*? Then choose the correct words in the rules.

I've created a webpage.
She's visited a chat room.
They've used a webcam.
We haven't downloaded music.
He hasn't posted a message.

RULES

1 We form the present perfect with **be** / **have** + past participle.
2 Regular past participles end with **-ed** / **-ing**.
3 We can use the present perfect to talk about **experiences** / **plans** which we've had.

More practice ⇨ Workbook page 25

5 Write sentences using the present perfect affirmative and negative.

Our teacher (use) the Internet a lot today. ✘
Our teacher hasn't used the Internet a lot today.

1 We (create) a webpage for our school. ✔
2 I (post) any messages this week. ✘
3 She (look) at my blog. ✘
4 My friend (change) his e-mail address. ✔
5 I (chat) a lot today. ✘
6 We (download) that program. ✘
7 The Internet (change) the way we communicate. ✔
8 I (visit) a lot of music websites. ✔

6 ACTIVATE Write sentences about you and people you know. Use the present perfect. Then compare your answers with other people in the class.

(visit) the U.S.
My dad has visited the U.S.

1 (appear) on YouTube
2 (live) in another country
3 (download) movies
4 (create) a blog
5 (travel) by plane
6 (play) a musical instrument

My dad has visited the U.S.

Luke and Pat haven't lived in another country, but our teacher has lived in England.

Finished?
Write about how much time you spend doing different things online / on a computer.

READING ■ Internet addiction

I can understand a text about Internet addiction.

1 **Read the title of the article. What do you think it means to be *trapped in the net*?**

STUDY STRATEGY ▢ Matching headings with paragraphs

2 1.38 **Read the text and underline words and ideas that go with headings a–e. Then match the headings with paragraphs 1–4. There is one heading that you do not need. Then listen and check your answers.**

a Online gamer
b Do something about it
c Stolen identity
d A new identity
e Serious symptoms

3 **Complete the summary of the text with six of the words in the box.**

plays games	messages	online	Internet
chat rooms	real	virtual	psychologists

This article describes two people's experience of the [1]___. Jenny spends time in a [2]___ community, while Tom [3]___ online. These days, some people spend more time in [4]___ and on game sites than with their [5]___ friends. It's a problem which [6]___ have now identified and which they can treat.

4 **BUILD YOUR VOCABULARY Find the nouns in the text that go with these verbs.**

fight	make	~~turn on~~	play	recognize
feel	spend			

turn on – laptop

5 **Complete the sentences with the correct form of the verbs in exercise 4. What are the new collocations?**

Can you ***turn on*** the TV, please?

1 I'm sure I ___ the man by the door.
2 I ___ angry when I lose a game.
3 I can't ___ any more money.
4 My sister ___ the piano very well.
5 They always ___ a lot of noise.
6 They ___ their enemies.

6 **YOUR OPINIONS Ask and answer the questions.**

1 Do you know anyone who has similar problems to those described in the text?
2 How do they behave?
3 How do you use the Internet?
4 Do you think you spend too much time on the Internet? Why / Why not?
5 What are the positive and negative sides of the Internet?

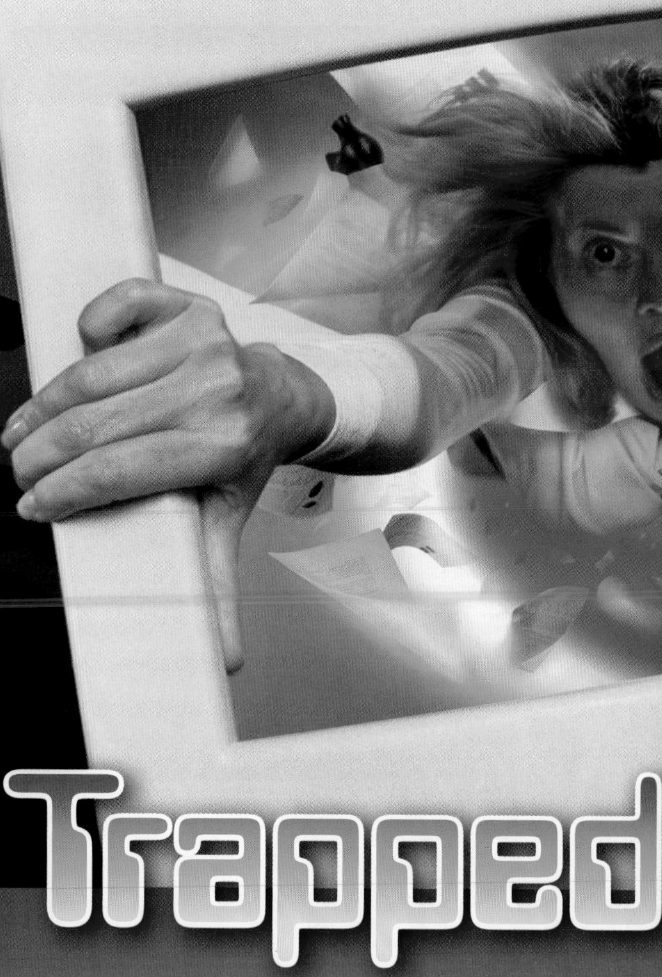

1 Jenny Foxton is a high school student, but she also has another life. She spends all night on the net. Every night she turns on her laptop and visits a virtual world called *Habbo*, where users have created avatars, rooms and communities. Jenny's avatar has bought clothes and also furniture for her room, using virtual money. When she isn't buying virtual possessions, her avatar moves from place to place, chatting to some of the millions of people who have joined *Habbo* around the world.

2 Tom Dobson's life on the Internet is different, but also very time-consuming and obsessive. At two or three o'clock in the morning, Tom is often fighting battles with ogres on his computer. Tom hasn't slept. His mother made him a sandwich seven hours ago, but he hasn't eaten it. He's one of eleven million people who play *World of Warcraft* online. His battle continues …

in the net

It can be cool to blog, chat, or play games online, but when you've been on the Internet for forty-eight hours non-stop, or more than a hundred hours a week, your idea of reality changes. This can happen to real addicts, who often feel tired, depressed, and isolated. Most people use the Internet sensibly, but between five and ten percent of Internet users are addicted to the web, and psychologists now recognize this as a problem.

Internet addiction has ruined people's education, relationships, and careers. It's now one of the main reasons why college students fail. If you've ever spent more time online than offline, maybe it's time to come back to real life and find some help. There are clinics, advice, and cures if you have a problem. And a lot of them are online, of course.

1 Complete the table with the past participle form of the verbs in the box. Then check your answers in the text.

~~create~~ buy join sleep eat be ruin spend

Regular (ends in *-ed*)	Irregular (doesn't end in *-ed*)
create – created	

More practice ⇨ Workbook page 25

2 Add the verbs in the box to the table in exercise 1.

have find sell write speak stay design put play go make visit

Pronunciation: Vowels ⇨ Workbook page 90

3 1.39 Listen to a conversation. Write a check mark for things that the speakers have done and put a cross for things they haven't done.

	Mark	Mary	Paul
online war games	✔		
clothes online			
virtual world			
an avatar			
friends online			
DVDs and books			
all night			

4 1.39 Work in pairs and write sentences about Mark, Mary, and Paul using verbs from exercises 1 and 2. Then listen again and check.

Mary has created an avatar.

Mark hasn't visited a virtual world.

5 ACTIVATE Compare your Internet use with a partner. Then tell the class about your partner's Internet use. Use the ideas from exercises 3 and 4.

I've never spent three hours online without a break.

Alan has visited a virtual world.

Finished?

Write about five things you haven't done on the Internet. Write why you haven't done them.

I haven't used a webcam. I don't have a webcam.

VOCABULARY AND LISTENING ■ Cybercrime

I can talk about cybercrime.

1 **Check the meaning of the words in the box. Then complete the dialogue with six of the words.**

> hacker virus antivirus software inbox password firewall spam phishing spam filter

Sam Do you get a lot of spam? I've had thirty junk e-mails in my [1]___ today!

Jane I have a [2]___, so I don't get many. But I got a bad [3]___ last week. I couldn't open my files. My [4]___ didn't block it. I really need to change it.

Sam I've received an e-mail asking me to update my bank details. What do you think?

Jane That's a typical [5]___ technique. Don't open it and put it in the trash. Oh, and change your [6]___, too!

2 1.40 **Read presentation texts 1–3. Listen to the radio program and choose the correct text.**

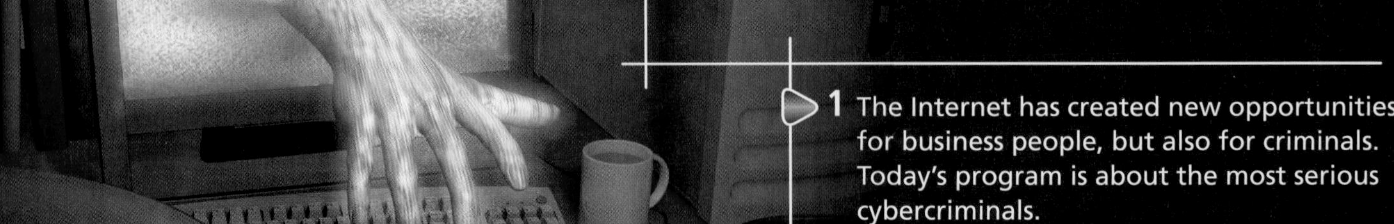

1 The Internet has created new opportunities for business people, but also for criminals. Today's program is about the most serious cybercriminals.

2 Has your computer ever had a virus? Have you received spam? These are just two problems we discuss on today's program.

3 The Internet is useful, but it's also a dangerous place. On today's program, we interview a computer hacker.

3 1.40 **Listen again and choose the correct answers.**

1 When is the program?
   a 9:00 a.m. b 11:00 a.m. c 8:00 p.m.

2 Which is Dr. Smith?

a  b  c 

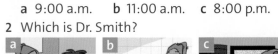

3 What is Elena's problem?

a 

b 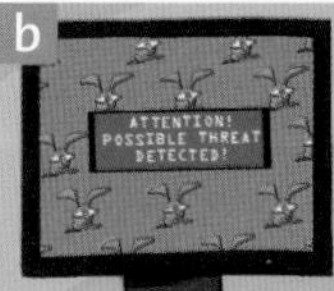

c 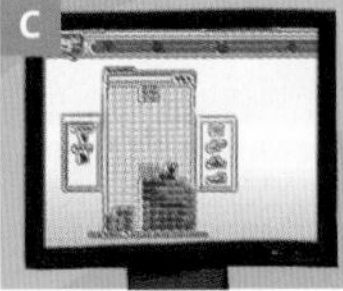

4 What was Bridget's password?
   a 12031998 b Mq43hIM00 c 12345678

5 Which problem do they not discuss on the program?
   a phishing b spam c hackers

6 Who is likely to find this radio program most useful?
   a computer scientists b cybercriminals
   c ordinary people who use computers

4 ACTIVATE **Ask and answer the questions.**

1 Have you ever had problems with a virus? If so, what happened? If not, what can viruses do?
2 Have you ever answered a spam e-mail? What happened?
3 What do you use passwords for? How many do you have?
4 Do you receive a lot of spam? What do you do with it?
5 What do you think are the most serious cybercrimes?

LANGUAGE FOCUS ■ Present perfect: questions

I can ask and answer about experiences.

3

1 **Complete the sentences from the listening on page 32 with the words in the box. How do you say *ever* in your language? What is the opposite of *ever*?**

attacked 's ~~Have~~ have Has

Have you ever received spam?

1 Has a hacker ___ your computer?
2 ___ your computer had a virus?
3 What problems ___ you had?
4 What ___ happened to you?

More practice ⇨ Workbook page 27

2 **Order the words to make questions. Then write answers for the questions.**

1 you / visited / what / websites / recently / have
2 any music / recently / downloaded / your friends / have
3 you / have / on the Internet / put / that picture / why
4 lost / ever / a computer file / you / have
5 she / visited / a chat room / has / ever
6 have / written / what / they / on the message board

3 **Complete the questions using the present perfect. Then ask and answer with a partner.**

1 (you read) any good jokes on the Internet?
2 (a virus attack) your computer recently?
3 (your friend make) money on the Internet?
4 (your grandparents use) the Internet?
5 (you e-mail) someone recently?
6 (your teacher use) the Internet in class?

4 **Complete the dialogue with questions in the present perfect.**

Jenna [1]___ ___ ___ any money online?
Tony No, I haven't made any money, but I've won things in competitions.
Jenna What [2]___ ___ ___?
Tony Oh, computer games, a webcam. Things like that.
Jenna [3]___ ___ ___ your own blog?
Tony Yes, I've created a blog with pictures.
Jenna How many people [4]___ ___ it?
Tony Nearly two hundred people have visited it. It's very good.
Jenna [5]___ ___ ___ any interesting people online?
Tony Yes, I've met a lot of hackers.
Jenna Hackers! [6]___ ___ ___ anything?
Tony No, I haven't stolen anything, but I've read some very secret files!

5 **Study the key phrases. Number a–e in order of frequency: 1 = never, 5 = very frequent.**

KEY PHRASES ○ Experiences

Have you ever ... ?
a Yes, occasionally. ___
b Yes, a lot of times. ___
c No, never. 1
d Yes, a few times. ___
e Yes, once (or twice). ___
What about you?

6 **ACTIVATE** **Find someone who has done 1–8. Ask and answer questions using the key phrases.**

Have you ever won an online competition?

No, I haven't. What about you?

1 (win) an online competition
2 (send) jokes to friends by e-mail
3 (have) a bad online experience
4 (have) problems with a virus
5 (buy) clothes on the Internet
6 (write) a blog
7 (meet) people in a chat room
8 (copy) homework from a website

○ *Finished?*

Write true sentences about your friends' answers in exercise 6.

Maria has never won an online competition.

SPEAKING ■ Apologizing and explaining

I can apologize for something and explain how it happened.

1 **Look at the picture. How long do you think Lucy has been on the computer?**

2 1.41 **Listen to the dialogue. Why hasn't Lucy slept all night?**

Mom	Look at the time! Have you been up all night?
Lucy	Yes. Listen, Mom, I have something to tell you.
Mom	What is it? What's the matter?
Lucy	I've done something really stupid.
Mom	What have you done?
Lucy	I'm afraid I've lost your file with the pictures.
Mom	You mean the file with the vacation pictures?
Lucy	Yes. Sorry, Mom. I didn't mean to. I don't know how it happened. I've been up all night looking for it.
Mom	Well, I've got a back-up copy, but you know I don't like it when you use my computer.
Lucy	I'm really sorry.
Mom	Please ask me next time. And try to be more careful.
Lucy	Don't worry. It won't happen again, I promise.

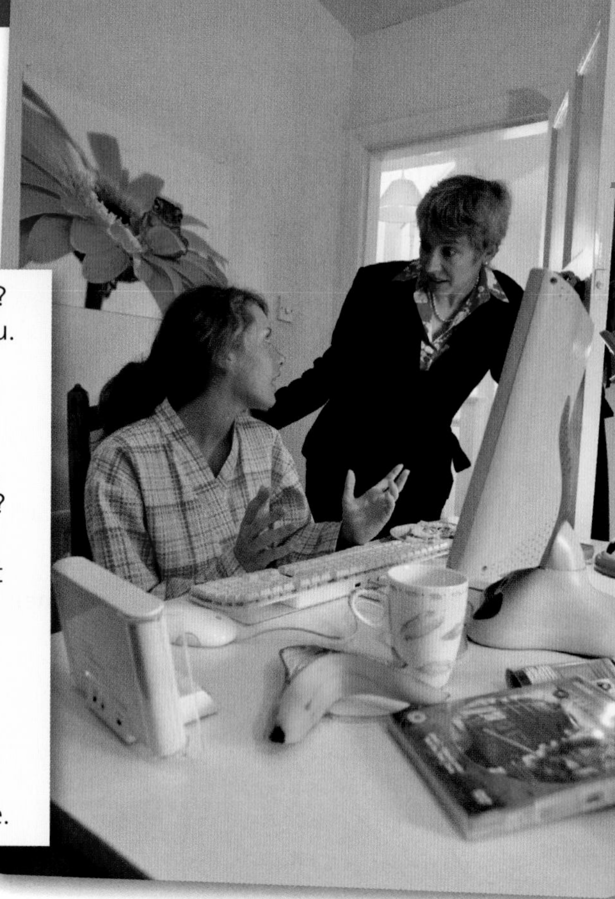

3 1.42 **Complete the key phrases with the words in the box. Who says them? Listen and check. Then practice the dialogue with a partner.**

don't mean worry sorry matter happen

KEY PHRASES ○ Apologizing and explaining

What is it?	I [3]___ know how it happened.
What's the [1]___?	I'm really [4]___.
I'm afraid … .	Don't [5]___.
I didn't [2]___ to.	It won't [6]___ again.

4 **Match sentences 1–8 with pictures A–D.**

1 Have you broken it?
2 Please ask next time you want to use my bike.
3 I didn't know your camera was there.
4 It's the second time that you've crashed it!
5 This is the second DVD you've lost.
6 Have you crashed it again?
7 Have you used all my free minutes?
8 You know I don't like it when you use my cell phone.

5 **Work in pairs. Reply to the sentences in exercise 4.**

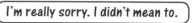

Have you broken it?

I'm really sorry. I didn't mean to.

6 **ACTIVATE** **Prepare a new dialogue with a partner. Use one of the pictures A–D. Practice your dialogue. Then choose another picture and change roles.**

WRITING ■ A comment on a website

I can write an opinion comment on a website.

3

Nearly 80 percent of young people in the U.S. use the Internet every day. What do they do online? Is Internet addiction really a problem? E-zine wants to know your opinions.

Post a comment | Report to moderator

I go on the Internet every day, but I've never spent more than an hour at a time online. I have a laptop and also a smartphone, so I can use the Internet anywhere. Today, for instance, I've been online three times.

Mainly, I just e-mail friends. I read online magazines and I look for information, too. I also compare prices of things, but I've never bought anything online because I don't think it's safe.

I'm not an Internet addict, but some of my friends are. One friend always looks tired because he spends all night online. Although he's failed a lot of tests, he hasn't changed his habits. In my experience, the Internet is not the only addictive activity. Another friend spends all her time watching TV!

In conclusion, from what I've seen, people can be obsessive about anything. However, I think that the Internet is definitely more addictive than some other things. The problem is that people can go online anywhere, at any time. For this reason, I think it is a more serious addiction. In my opinion, the real problem is with the person, not with the activity. These people need help.

Sean (15)

1 Read the model text and answer the questions.

1 Who is the writer of this text?
2 Who are the readers?
3 How often does the writer go online?
4 Does he know any Internet addicts?
5 What is the real problem behind addictive habits?

2 Complete the key phrases. Then read the model text again and check.

KEY PHRASES ○ Expressing opinions

... in [1]___ experience	The [3]___ is that ... .
... from what I've [2]___, ...	For this [4]___, I think ... .
I think	In my opinion, ...

Language point: Addition and contrast linkers

3 Study the words in blue in the model text. Then put these words into two groups.

Adding ideas	Contrast
also	

4 Complete the sentences with the words in exercise 3.

1 I watch a lot of TV, ___ I prefer watching DVDs.
2 He plays computer games and he visits chat rooms, ___.
3 I have a blog and ___ a personal website.
4 Computer games are fun. ___, I think they are addictive.
5 ___ Facebook is popular, I prefer Twitter.
6 I send e-mails, ___ I don't visit chat rooms.

5 ACTIVATE Follow the steps in the writing guide.

○ WRITING GUIDE

A TASK

Write a comment with your opinion about the discussion topic in the model text.

B THINK AND PLAN

1 How often do you use the Internet and how long do you spend online at a time?
2 How do you use the Internet?
3 Do you know anyone who uses the Internet a lot? Has this had bad consequences?
4 Do you know people who are obsessive about other activities? What activities?
5 Do you think that the Internet is more or less addictive than TV or other activities? Why / Why not?
6 What can people do if they're using the Internet too much?

C WRITE

Paragraph 1: Write about your Internet use
I go on the Internet ...
Paragraph 2: Describe your online habits
My main activity on the Internet is ...
Paragraph 3: Describe other people's habits
Some of my friends are ...
Paragraph 4: Conclusion
In conclusion, ...

D CHECK

- phrases for expressing opinions
- addition and contrast linkers
- present perfect

REVIEW Unit 3

Vocabulary

1 Complete the sentences with the words in the box.

download	online games	posted	engines
e-mail	webpage	blog	message

1 Have you received an ___ from your brother recently?
2 Can you help me ___ this music?
3 Do you ___ people or send e-mails?
4 I've created a ___ and friends can leave comments on it.
5 My sister plays ___ all the time.
6 A friend ___ a message on my blog.
7 What search ___ do you use?
8 I've posted pictures of my dog on my personal ___.

2 Choose the correct words.

1 A **hacker** / **virus** is a type of online criminal.
2 I use **spam** / **antivirus software** to protect my computer.
3 You can stop a lot of **spam** / **hackers** with a filter.
4 It's a good idea to change your **software** / **password** pretty often.
5 A **firewall** / **virus** is a dangerous computer program.
6 I have **a firewall** / **an inbox** to protect against phishing.

Language focus

3 Write affirmative or negative sentences using the present perfect.

1 My mom / create / a blog
2 My friend / send / me / a lot of e-mails
3 We / not download / videos
4 I / play / an online game once
5 My grandparents / not use / the Internet
6 My friends / make / money on the Internet / a few times

4 Write questions and short answers for the sentences in exercise 3. Use *ever*.

Has your mom ever created a blog?
Yes, she has.

Communication

5 Match sentences 1–8 with responses a–h.

1 What have you done?
2 You've lost the file with my pictures?
3 What have you bought online recently?
4 This isn't the first time you've downloaded a virus.
5 Have you ever lost a file?
6 What's the matter?
7 What about you?
8 Have your friends ever downloaded videos?

a Yes, a lot of times.
b I never go on the Internet!
c Some new antivirus software.
d I'm sorry. It won't happen again.
e A virus has attacked my computer.
f I've lost my mom's file.
g Yes, I'm really sorry. I didn't mean to.
h Yes, I have. But only once.

Listening

6 1.43 **Listen to an interview with a computer hacker and complete the notes.**

Mr. X is [1]___ and he goes to a public high school. He's [2]___ years old and he became a computer [3]___ and started hacking when he was [4]___.

Hackers use small [5]___, which they write themselves, to get inside other people's computers. Hackers do this mainly for [6]___ and not to steal information. Hackers don't usually target private computers because the security is very [7]___ to break. Mr. X has never sold any [8]___. He has visited government networks [9]___ and his dad's company [10]___.

PROJECT A website plan

3

1 Read the website plan. Match links 1–4 with pages A–D.

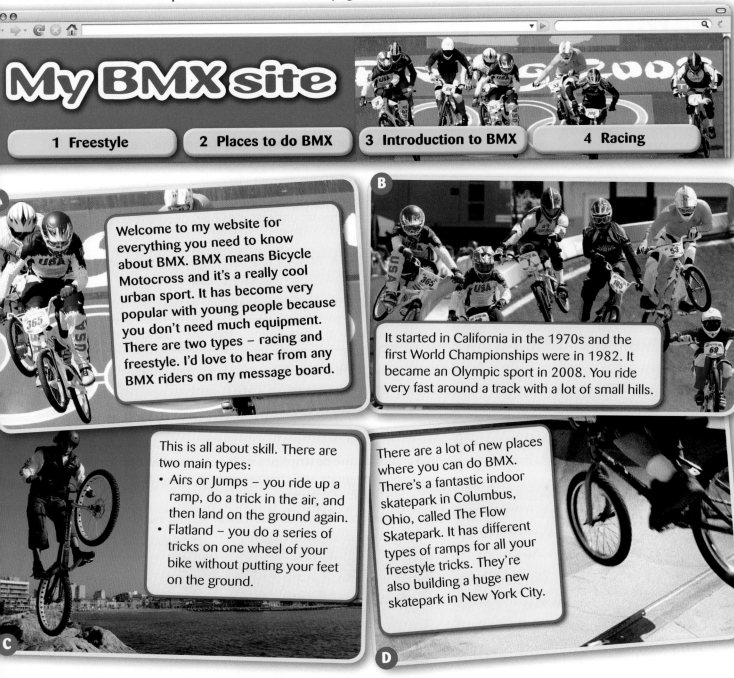

1 Freestyle | 2 Places to do BMX | 3 Introduction to BMX | 4 Racing

A

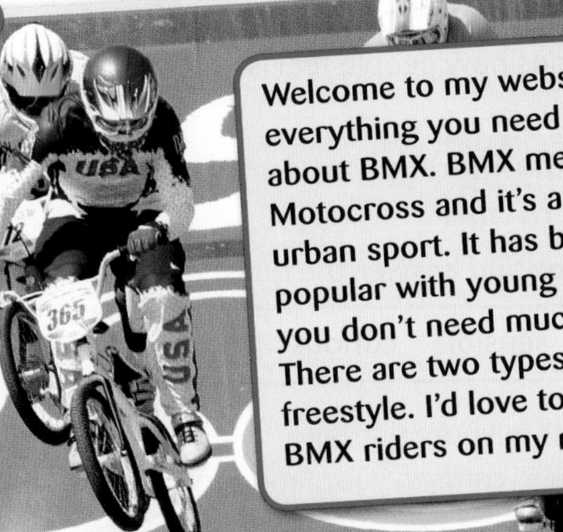

Welcome to my website for everything you need to know about BMX. BMX means Bicycle Motocross and it's a really cool urban sport. It has become very popular with young people because you don't need much equipment. There are two types – racing and freestyle. I'd love to hear from any BMX riders on my message board.

B

It started in California in the 1970s and the first World Championships were in 1982. It became an Olympic sport in 2008. You ride very fast around a track with a lot of small hills.

C

This is all about skill. There are two main types:

- Airs or Jumps – you ride up a ramp, do a trick in the air, and then land on the ground again.
- Flatland – you do a series of tricks on one wheel of your bike without putting your feet on the ground.

D

There are a lot of new places where you can do BMX. There's a fantastic indoor skatepark in Columbus, Ohio, called The Flow Skatepark. It has different types of ramps for all your freestyle tricks. They're also building a huge new skatepark in New York City.

2 Make a website plan. Follow the steps in the project checklist.

PROJECT CHECKLIST

1. Think of an activity that you do in your free time, or something that you're interested in.
2. Plan the contents of your website. Think about: places in your area to do the activity, details about it, equipment you need, and famous people who do it.
3. Write a home page for your website. Include an introduction to the activity, a few important dates, why it has become popular, and some links to other pages.
4. Write a short text for each page.
5. Find pictures for your website plan on the Internet or in a magazine.

3 Share your website plan with the rest of the class. Which activity do you want to try?

Fame

Start thinking

1 What is face reading?
2 What is celebrity culture?
3 What is LaGuardia Arts?

Aims

Communication: I can...

- describe people's personalities.
- understand a text about fame.
- talk about things that people have done.
- understand an interview about a creative school.
- talk about things I have read, heard, or seen.
- identify and describe people.
- write a biography of a celebrity.

Vocabulary

- Adjectives: personality
- Nouns and adjectives: personal qualities

Language focus

- Adverbs of degree
- Present perfect + *still*, *yet*, *just*, and *already*
- *for* and *since*
- Present perfect and simple past

Reach Out Options

Extra listening and speaking
Describing people
Page 91

Curriculum extra
Language and literature: Newspapers
Page 99

Culture
Teenage magazines
Page 107

Vocabulary bank
Prefixes and suffixes; Music
Page 115

VOCABULARY AND LANGUAGE FOCUS
Adjectives: personality
I can describe people's personalities.

1 2.06 **Check the meaning of the words in blue in the *Face reading guide*. Then complete the sentences with adjectives. Listen and check.**

1 A person who likes investigating things is ___.
2 A person who likes being busy in his or her free time is ___.
3 A person who doesn't like meeting new people is ___.
4 A person who wants to be successful is ___.
5 A person who doesn't have much experience of the world is ___.
6 A person who doesn't like giving money to people is ___.
7 A person who doesn't accept other people's ideas is ___.
8 A person who understands how people feel is ___.

STUDY STRATEGY Identifying cognates and false friends

2 Study the words in the box and answer the questions.

practical intelligent sensible curious active

1 Are there similar words in your language?
2 Are the meanings of the words in your language similar or different?

3 Look at the descriptions of the faces below. Use the *Face reading guide* and choose the best words in the texts. Then justify your answers.

I think Scarlett Johansson is friendly because she has a round face.

Scarlett Johansson

Description:
Face: pretty round
Eyebrows: curved
Eyes: oval, pretty wide apart
Mouth: large, round

Analysis:
She's a very 1**friendly / shy** woman who can be a little 2**curious / intolerant** sometimes. She's cheerful and 3**practical / intelligent**. She's very 4**generous / stingy** and sensitive.

Daniel Craig

Description:
Face: square
Nose: wide
Eyebrows: heavy, straight
Eyes: oval

Analysis:
He's usually really 5**determined / innocent** and 6**shy / confident.** He's pretty 7**serious / cheerful**, 8**active / not very active**, and he's also 9**intolerant / intelligent**.

Adverbs of degree

4 **Choose the correct adverbs. What is the position of the adverbs in these sentences?**

1 It's **incredibly** / **a little** difficult. Nobody can do it.
2 He's **not very** / **pretty** tolerant. He doesn't like many of my friends.
3 Is that Amy singing? I thought she **wasn't very** / **was really** shy!
4 A million dollars for me? You're **a little** / **very** generous.
5 Sam **is a little** / **isn't very** sensitive. Don't say bad things about him.
6 Liam **is incredibly** / **isn't very** tall – over two meters!

More practice ⇨ Workbook page 33

5 **Rewrite the sentences with the correct adverbs.**

I hated that movie. It was bad. (really / a little)
I hated that movie. It was really bad.
1 One dollar! That's stingy! (a little / not very)
2 It's a fantastic place. I'm happy that we're here. (a little / really)
3 That new Ferrari is expensive. (pretty / not very)
4 They get up at 6 a.m. That's early. (incredibly / pretty)
5 He's a big Chicago Bulls fan. He thinks that they're good. (really / not very)

6 **Study the key phrases. Then think of two people and complete the key phrases for each person. Use different adverbs of degree.**

KEY PHRASES ◻ Describing people

She tends to be (pretty) ... .
He can be (very) ... .
He's sometimes / always (a little) ... .
He isn't (very) ... .
My (aunt) can be (incredibly) ... .

7 **ACTIVATE Work in pairs. Take turns to describe and guess famous people or someone you both know. Use the key phrases and adverbs of degree.**

This person tends to be a little shy. He can be very generous and he's always very cheerful.

I think it's John.

◻ Finished?
Write a short description of one of the people you discussed in exercise 7.

FACE READING GUIDE

FACE	**Round:** friendly sensitive	**Square:** ambitious determined	**Triangular:** intelligent	**Long:** practical sensible
EYEBROWS	**Heavy:** serious	**Thin:** not very confident	**Curved:** curious	**Straight:** active
EYES	**Round:** innocent	**Oval:** intelligent	**Wide apart:** tolerant	**Close together:** intolerant
NOSE	**Wide:** confident	**Small:** shy	**Long:** curious	**Short:** cheerful
MOUTH	**Round:** sensitive	**Large:** generous	**Narrow:** stingy	

READING ■ Celebrity culture

I can understand a text about fame.

1 **Check the meaning of the words in blue in the text. Then read the title of the text. What do you think *instant fame* means? How can people become instantly famous?**

2 2.07 **Read and listen to the text and check your answers in exercise 1.**

3 **Read the text again and choose the correct answers.**

1 What type of text is this?
   a A critical article about fame.
   b A review of a talent show.
   c A description of famous people.
2 Who is Craig Jones?
   a a celebrity
   b a talent show participant
   c a fashion model
3 How does Craig feel about the outcome of his audition?
   a positive
   b negative
   c he doesn't know
4 What can you read about in gossip magazines?
   a talent surveys
   b soccer players
   c models
5 Who benefits from the creation of these new stars?
   a the entertainment industry
   b the young artists
   c the record companies

4 **BUILD YOUR VOCABULARY Study the prefixes and suffixes in blue. Then complete definitions 1–5 with the words in the box. There is one word that you do not need.**

can can't across the whole with without not

1 pointless – ___ a point
2 uncreative – ___ creative
3 nationwide – ___ nation
4 successful – ___ success
5 disposable – you ___ dispose of this.

5 **Complete the sentences. Add the prefixes or suffixes in exercise 4 to the words in the box. There is one word that you do not need.**

kind use create world sleep predict

1 Thanks for the advice. I think it'll be very ___.
2 I'm very tired. I had a ___ night.
3 I know what he will do. He's usually pretty ___.
4 Don't be ___. Give your sister some of the chocolate.
5 The song was a ___ hit.

6 **YOUR OPINIONS Ask and answer the questions.**

1 Why are people obsessed with celebrities?
2 Do normal people become famous very often?
3 Why do some stars have long careers?
4 Which TV programs create celebrities?
5 Have you ever seen a celebrity? Who? Where?

Instant Fame

New celebrities seem to appear every day. But who creates these stars and for how long are they famous?

It's 9 a.m. and Craig Jones has just arrived outside a building where nearly a thousand hopeful young singers and dancers are standing in line to audition for a talent show. Two hours later, Craig still hasn't gone inside the building. He's already auditioned for two other shows this year without success, but he hasn't given up yet. He's changed his act and he's confident that this time will be his big break.

This is the age of the celebrity. Gossip magazines are full of Hollywood stars and fashion models, and talent shows discover a new star nearly every week. It seems that anybody can become an overnight sensation. A survey has found that one in six young Americans really believes that they can become rich and famous if they win a talent show, but the reality is very different.

For the winners of talent shows, life isn't easy. They sign a contract and have a hit with their song from the show. But the second and third hits are more difficult, and music is an expensive business. It costs about $6,500 to record a song, $40,000 to advertise it, and between $50,000 and $1,300,000 to make a good video. Then they must pay their manager about 20 percent.

Creating celebrities is a profitable business for the entertainment industry, but not many of these artists become rich and famous. Most of them are one-hit wonders who disappear from the public eye when the media "discovers" the next big star. For these wannabe celebrities, the return to normal life is very hard. "Celebrity Street" is often a dead end. Fame can be instant, but it can also finish fast.

LANGUAGE FOCUS ■ Present perfect + *still*, *yet*, *just*, and *already*

I can talk about things that people have done.

4

1 Complete the sentences from the text. Then match sentences 1–4 with a or b.

1 Craig Jones has ___ arrived.
2 Craig ___ hasn't gone inside the building.
3 He's ___ auditioned for two other shows.
4 He hasn't given up ___.

a This describes an action which hasn't happened.
b This describes an action which has happened.

More practice ⇨ Workbook page 33

2 Complete the rules with *still*, *yet*, *just*, and *already*.

RULES

1 We use **still** with negative sentences. It goes before *hasn't* / *haven't*.
2 We use ___ and ___ with affirmative sentences. They go between *has* / *have* and the verb.
3 We use ___ with questions and negative sentences. It goes at the end of the sentence.

3 Order the words to make sentences.

1 they / haven't / still / made / the video
2 we / have / already / the talent show / seen
3 already / they've / two hits / had
4 won / she / a talent show / just / has
5 you / yet / signed / a contract / have / ?
6 seen / just / a really good / I've / movie
7 the actor / hasn't / still / found / a job

4 Write answers for the questions with *still*, *yet*, *just*, and *already*. Use your own ideas.

Why are you smiling? (just)
Because I've just had some good news.
1 Why isn't your friend here? (still)
2 Why is your friend happy? (just)
3 Why aren't the students working? (yet)
4 Why are you going to the movies? (yet)
5 Why aren't you having lunch? (already)
6 Why aren't they at school? (still)

5 2.08 ACTIVATE **Listen to six dialogues and write sentences for 1–6 with the verbs in the box. Use *still*, *yet*, *just*, and *already*. Then ask and answer with a partner.**

finish see make find write arrive

1 Cody / dinner
2 Simon / at school
3 Polly / her essay
4 John / the test
5 Haley / the movie
6 Joe / a job

Has Cody made dinner yet?

No, he hasn't. He hasn't decided what to make.

Finished?

Write sentences about your day using *still*, *yet*, *just*, and *already*.

I've already had two classes today.

VOCABULARY AND LISTENING ■ Nouns and adjectives: personal qualities

I can understand an interview about a creative school.

1 Check the meanings of the words in blue. Then read the text and choose the correct words.

LaGuardia Arts

LaGuardia Arts, a public high school in New York, mixes academic lessons with [1]creative / intelligent subjects, like art, drama, and media studies. People with a lot of [2]talent / good looks have studied there, like Jennifer Aniston, Nicki Minaj, and Robert De Niro, but people there say that it isn't a [3]"fame / style school." The school wants to help its students to be [4]skillful / egotistical and [5]lucky / independent. Students there usually have their feet on the ground and don't have big [6]egos / strengths. It's a large school, but people feel [7]lucky / courageous if they can study there.

2 2.09 Complete the table with words in exercise 1. Then listen and check.

Nouns	Adjectives
1___	talented
2___	stylish
creativity	3___
4___	good-looking
intelligence	5___
6___	famous
luck	7___
ego	8___
skill	9___
independence	10___
11___	strong
courage	12___

Barack Obama

Emma Watson

Prince William

Rihanna

Rafael Nadal

3 2.10 Listen to an interview with Troy and Stacey. Who are they?

a Ex-students of LaGuardia Arts.
b Big stars in Britain.
c Students at LaGuardia Arts.

4 2.10 Listen again and write *true* or *false*. Correct the false sentences.

1 Troy has been at LaGuardia Arts since he was 14.
2 Troy's specialty is art.
3 The school teaches students to be sensible and realistic.
4 It is very difficult to get a place at the school.
5 Stacey started at the school three years ago.
6 Stacey has just made a CD.

5 Which of the key phrases can you complete with a noun and which with an adjective? Look at the pictures. What qualities are important for the different professions?

You need a lot of style to be an actress.

KEY PHRASES ○ Talking about qualities

He's / She's really / very / not exactly [1]___.
He / She has / doesn't have (a lot of) [2]___.
You need (a lot of) [3]___.
You don't need (much) [4]___ to be a (singer).
It's important for a (tennis player) to be [5]___.
A (sports) star needs / doesn't need to be [6]___.

6 ACTIVATE Play a guessing game. Write sentences about the jobs in the box using key phrases. Then work in pairs and guess the jobs.

astronaut movie director model poet soccer player opera singer politician

You need a lot of courage to do this. It is also important to be intelligent.

I know! An astronaut.

LANGUAGE FOCUS ■ *for* and *since* • Present perfect and simple past

I can talk about things I have read, heard, or seen.

4

for and *since*

1 **Choose the correct words in sentences 1–3 from the listening on page 42. Then match the sentences with descriptions a and b in the rules.**

1 I've been here **since** / **for** 2008.
2 He's been here **since** / **for** he was 14.
3 I've been here **since** / **for** a year.

RULES

a This tells us the point when a state or action begins.
b This tells us the duration of a state or action.

More practice ⇨ Workbook page 35

2 **Work in pairs. Decide which time expressions go with *for* and which go with *since*. Then add two more time expressions to each group.**

two years · last Saturday · an hour · March · a long time · Christmas · I met him · 2009 · a month · two days

3 **Complete the sentences using the present perfect form of the verbs in parentheses and *for* or *since*.**

1 We ___ Brad ___ three weeks. (not see)
2 Our school ___ here ___ 1990. (be)
3 That singer ___ a big ego ___ she appeared on TV. (have)
4 I ___ a good song ___ a long time. (not hear)
5 They ___ a CD ___ two years. (not release)
6 This is my lucky pen. I ___ it ___ months. (have)

4 **Complete the sentences with *for* or *since* and your own ideas. Then work in pairs and ask and answer questions with *How long ...?***

1 I've studied English ___.
2 We've been at this school ___.
3 My family has lived in this city ___.
4 This school has been here ___.
5 My friend has had a computer ___.
6 I've liked sports ___.

How long have you studied English?

I've studied English since I was 11.

Present perfect and simple past

5 **Study the examples and answer the questions.**

a I've learned a lot this year.
b I studied here three years ago.
c He's studied at the school since 2008.
d He started at this school last year.
e How long have you lived here?
f When did you see *Avatar*?

1 Which sentences are in the present perfect tense and which are in the simple past?
2 Which sentences describe an action that started and finished in the past?
3 Which sentences describe an action that still continues in the present?

More practice ⇨ Workbook page 35

6 **Complete the text with the correct form of the verbs in parentheses. Use the present perfect or the simple past.**

Victoria and David Beckham [1]___ (have) very successful, but very different, careers. They first [2]___ (meet) in 1997, when David [3]___ (play) soccer for Manchester United. At that time, Victoria [4]___ (be) a singer in the Spice Girls. David and Victoria [5]___ (get) married in 1999.

Victoria and David [6]___ (have) four children. They [7]___ (be) in the public eye since they [8]___ (meet).

7 **ACTIVATE** **Write things that you have read, heard, or seen this month. Then work in pairs and ask and answer questions.**

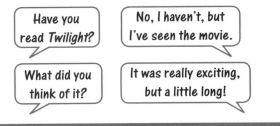

Have you read Twilight?

No, I haven't, but I've seen the movie.

What did you think of it?

It was really exciting, but a little long!

Finished?

Write four sentences about things you have done and places you have visited. Write when you did the activities.

I've visited Mexico City. I went there last summer.

SPEAKING ■ Identifying and describing people

I can identify and describe people.

1 **Describe the people in the picture. What are they wearing? What are they doing?**

2 2.11 **Listen to the dialogue. Who's Adam looking at?**

Lucy	Who are you looking at, Adam?
Adam	Oh, hi, Lucy. Who's that girl over there? I think I've seen her before.
Lucy	Which one? The girl with long hair?
Adam	No, the tall girl with the blue jeans. She's talking on the phone.
Lucy	Oh, that's Joanna Mills. What about her?
Adam	Do you know her, then?
Lucy	Yes, she goes to our school, but she hasn't been there long. She started in September. Why?
Adam	She looks like someone famous. She has an interesting face. Is she a model or a singer or something?
Lucy	No she isn't, Adam. She's just a normal student.
Adam	Oh, that's too bad. Never mind.

3 2.12 **Complete the key phrases from the dialogue. Who says them? Listen and check. Then practice the dialogue with a partner.**

KEY PHRASES ■ Identifying people

Who's that guy / girl [1]___ there?
I think I've seen him / her [2]___.
The guy / girl with [3]___?
What [4]___ him / her?
Do you [5]___ him / her?
He / She looks [6]___ someone famous.
He / She has [7]___.

Pronunciation: Vowels and diphthongs ⇨ Workbook page 91

4 **Imagine that you and a friend are looking at the people in the picture in exercise 6. Complete the sentences with the words in the box.**

shy seen blond smiling interesting blue T-shirt hair

1 The guy with the ___?
2 No, the guy with ___ hair and a green T-shirt.
3 She's ___ at the guy.
4 He has an ___ face.
5 Have you ___ her before?
6 Who's the girl with long curly ___?
7 The blond girl looks a little ___.

5 **Ask about people in your class. Describe hair, clothes, and location.**

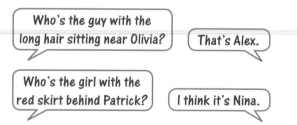

Who's the guy with the long hair sitting near Olivia?
That's Alex.
Who's the girl with the red skirt behind Patrick?
I think it's Nina.

6 **ACTIVATE Look at the picture below and practice a new dialogue with a partner.**

WRITING ■ A biography

I can write a biography of a celebrity.

4

1 Katheryn Elizabeth Hudson – "Katy Perry" – was born in Santa Barbara, California in 1984. As a singer, songwriter, and actress, Perry travels a lot, but she has lived in California all her life. Perry has a pretty face with long, black hair and lovely big blue eyes. She has a strong personality and she likes to wear brightly colored clothes.

2 Both of Perry's parents were pastors and Perry wasn't allowed to watch MTV or listen to pop music when she was a child. She sang in her church until she was 17. She released her first album of Christian music in 2001, but it wasn't very successful, and she had a hard time recording more albums.

3 She then started learning to write and sing pop songs. Her big break came in 2008 when she released her songs, *I Kissed a Girl* and *Hot n Cold*. In the years that followed, she released many other bestselling songs, including *California Girls*, *Teenage Dream*, and *Firework*.

4 Since then, Perry has become one of the most successful female artists in the world. She has won many awards and she has been involved in several movies, including a movie about her life called *Katy Perry: Part of Me*.

1 Read the model text and answer the questions.

1 Which paragraph describes Katy's teenage years?
2 What were Katy's parents like?
3 What kind of music was on her first album?
4 What happened in 2008?
5 What other work has she done in addition to singing?

2 Study the key phrases. Put the phrases in the order of the text. Then check your answers.

KEY PHRASES ○ A biography

She has ... and ... .
In the years that followed, ...
She's been involved in ... .
... was born in ... .
Since then, she has ... .
Her big break came in ... .

Language point: Order of adjectives

3 Complete the table with adjectives from the model text. Then order the words in 1–6.

Opinion	Size / Length	Age	Color	Noun
	1 ___		2 ___	hair
	big	new		car
3 ___	4 ___		5 ___	eyes

1 She's a (shy / child / little).
2 She lives in a (apartment / new / big).
3 She has (long / hair / blond).
4 Her sister has (beautiful / eyes / big / brown).
5 She's a very (young / warm-hearted / girl).
6 She's wearing a (red / dress / lovely / long).

4 ACTIVATE Follow the steps in the writing guide.

○ WRITING GUIDE

A TASK

Write a biography of a famous actor, musician, or sports star.

B THINK AND PLAN

Find information about the person and make notes.

1 When and where was he / she born?
2 What does he / she look like?
3 When and how did he / she get involved in acting, music, or sports?
4 What was his / her first job?
5 When and how did he / she get a big break?
6 What happened after that?
7 What has happened since then?
8 How successful has the person been?
9 Has the person become famous for other things?

C WRITE

Paragraph 1: Personal information
... was born in ...
Paragraph 2: Studies
He / She studied ...
Paragraph 3: Success
His / Her big break came in ...
Paragraph 4: Recent career
Since then, he / she ...

D CHECK

• order of adjectives
• present perfect and simple past

Vocabulary

1 Match the words in the box with sentences 1–8.

ambitious sensitive cheerful tolerant serious generous stingy curious

1 She always gives things to her friends.
2 He wants to play soccer for his country.
3 She doesn't laugh very much.
4 My parents never give me any allowance.
5 Be careful what you say to her.
6 He smiles and laughs all the time.
7 My parents never stop me from doing things.
8 She always wants to know everything about everyone.

2 Make adjectives from these nouns.

1 style ___
2 skill ___
3 luck ___
4 talent ___
5 fame ___
6 creativity ___
7 independence ___
8 strength ___

Language focus

3 Complete the dialogue with the words in the box.

just yet (x2) already still (x2) for since

Miguel Have you done all your homework [1]___?
Sammy No, there's too much! I've worked on it [2]___ 8 p.m., but I [3]___ haven't finished it.
Miguel Have you finished the math exercises [4]___?
Sammy Yes, I've [5]___ done them, but I [6]___ haven't finished my English essay.
Miguel Well, I've [7]___ written the essay, but I haven't done the math exercises. I've worked on them [8]___ an hour, but I can't do them.
Sammy I know! I'll help you with the math exercises and you can help me with the essay.
Miguel Good idea!

4 Order the words to make sentences.

1 studied / long / you / how / have / English / ?
2 visited / yet / I / the U.S. / haven't
3 an interview / he / just / has / given
4 they / 1999 / lived / in Canada / have / since
5 brother / I / met / still / your / haven't
6 lived / for / they / twenty / here / have / years

5 Complete the text with the present perfect or the simple past form of the verbs in parentheses.

Britney Spears and Justin Timberlake [1]___ (be) friends for a long time. They first [2]___ (meet) on a TV show when Britney was eleven. When they were younger, they both [3]___ (sing) on a talent show. They [4]___ (not win), but since then they [5]___ (become) celebrities. In their careers, they [6]___ (have) a lot of hits. Justin [7]___ (have) his first hit in 1998 and Britney's first number one [8]___ (be) in 1999. They are good friends today, and they [9]___ (appear) together recently on TV and at concerts.

Communication

6 Complete the dialogue with the words in the box.

incredibly good-looking too bad a little tends short looks guy

Sarah What's your brother like?
Alison He can be [1]___ shy.
Sarah Who's the [2]___ with him? The tall guy with the [3]___ hair.
Alison Oh, that's Tony. What about him?
Sarah He [4]___ really nice.
Alison He is [5]___ nice, but he [6]___ to be a little serious.
Sarah He doesn't look serious. And he's very [7]___.
Alison Yes, and the girl with the long blond hair is his girlfriend.
Sarah That's [8]___! Never mind.

Listening

7 2.13 **Listen and choose the correct words.**

1 Beyoncé won **five / six** Grammy awards in 2010.
2 She won **a talent competition / a Grammy award** when she was seven.
3 Beyoncé first became a star in **1981 / 1997**.
4 She became **a solo singer / a member of Destiny's Child** in 2005.
5 She appeared in the movie *Dreamgirls* in **2004 / 2006**.
6 Her fashion company is called **Blue Ivy / House of Deréon**.

Listening

1 Look at the pictures and answer the questions.

1 Who are the celebrities?
2 Why are they famous?
3 What movies have some of the people been in?
4 Which person do you like best? Why?

2 2.14 **Listen to a conversation. Which celebrity in the photos do Joel and Ana not mention?**

3 2.14 **Listen again and complete the sentences.**

1 Joel and Ana saw a good ___ on TV last night.
2 Joel likes Angelina Jolie because he thinks she's the most ___ woman in the world.
3 Ana admires Jolie because she helps ___.
4 ___ gave a lot of money to help people in Haiti.
5 Joel says Shakira is very ___ and ___.
6 ___ favorite celebrity is David Beckham because he has done a lot for ___ people.
7 Ana admires Leonardo DiCaprio because he works with ___ groups.
8 Joel says Leonardo DiCaprio isn't as ___ as Beckham.

Speaking

4 Work in pairs and prepare a conversation about a celebrity you like. Imagine you have seen an interview with the celebrity on TV. Answer these questions.

1 Who did you see on TV?
2 What does he / she look like?
3 What has he / she done?
4 What other celebrities do you like? Why?
5 Who is your all-time favorite celebrity? Why?

5 Have a conversation. Use your ideas in exercise 4 and the chart below to help you. One of you is A and one of you is B. Change roles.

A *Did you see (name of celebrity) on ... ?*

B Reply.

A Comment on appearance. *He / She looks ... .*

B Comment on personality. *I think he / she is a ... person because ... .*

A Mention another celebrity. *Another person I ... . I admire him / her because ... .*

B Disagree.

A Ask about B's favorite celebrity. *Who is ... ?*

B Reply.

A Disagree.

B Reply.

Writing

6 Write a description of a person who you think is a good role model. Describe the person's appearance and character. Say what the person has done and why you admire him / her. Begin like this:

I've chosen ... as my role model. He / She is a ... person. I really admire this person because ... .

School life

Start thinking

1 What are different kinds of schools in the U.S.?
2 What's homeschooling?
3 How old are children when they leave school in your country?

Aims

Communication: I can ...

- talk about school rules.
- give my opinions about cheating at school.
- talk about rules at home and at school.
- understand people talking about schools.
- compare my school to schools in other countries.
- ask for and give advice.
- write an opinion essay.

Vocabulary

- School life: verbs
- School life: nouns

Language focus

- *should, must,* and *may not*
- *have to* and *don't have to*
- *should, must,* and *have to*

Reach Out Options

Extra listening and speaking

Talking about your school

Page 92

Curriculum extra

Citizenship: The school community

Page 100

Culture

Studying abroad

Page 108

Vocabulary bank

American vs. British English; School

Page 116

VOCABULARY AND LANGUAGE FOCUS

School life: verbs

I can talk about school rules.

1 Check the meaning of the words and phrases in blue in the *What's your attitude to school?* questionnaire. Then complete the table with the base form of the verbs.

Positive	Neutral	Negative
get good grades		

2 Work in pairs and do the questionnaire. Then check the key.

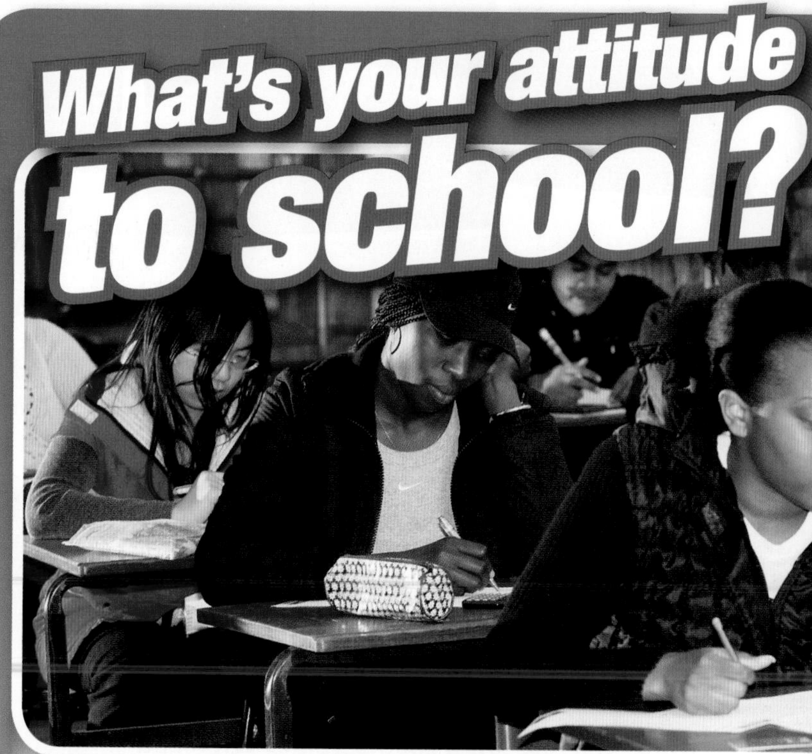
What's your attitude to school?

Are you a good student, or do you have an attitude problem?

1 What's the best way to enjoy school?
- **a** Make friends.
- **b** Get good grades and pass tests.
- **c** Both a and b.

2 What's the best way to avoid problems at school?
- **a** You should be truant.
- **b** You shouldn't be noisy in class.
- **c** You should study and help people.

3 When do you study for a test?
- **a** Never.
- **b** The day of the test.
- **c** A day or two before.

4 What do you think about people who cheat on tests?
- **a** It's normal.
- **b** People shouldn't do it, but it sometimes happens.
- **c** People may not cheat. It isn't allowed.

3 **Ask and answer the questions with a partner. Then compare your answers with the class.**

1 Did you do any homework last night? What was it?
2 Have you ever failed a test?
3 How do you feel before you take a test?
4 When did you last study for a test?
5 Do you usually get good grades in English?
6 Have you ever cheated on a test?
7 When are you going to leave school?
8 What do most people do after high school in your country?

5 If you fail a test, what should you do?
a Copy a friend's work next time.
b Do your homework in the future.
c Find out why you got a bad grade and take the test again.

6 What should you do if someone bullies you?
a You can't do anything.
b You should confront the bully.
c You must tell an adult about it.

7 What should schools do with bullies?
a Nothing.
b Suspend them or expel them.
c Write a polite letter to their parents.

8 What do you want to do before you leave school?
a Become more popular.
b Improve your English.
c Get a diploma.

Key
Mostly a: You have a bad attitude. You must try to be more positive.
Mostly b: Not bad. You don't have a bad attitude.
Mostly c: Well done! You have a good attitude to school and friends.

should, *must*, and *may not*

4 **Complete the sentences from the questionnaire. Then answer questions a–e.**

1 You ___ tell an adult about it.
2 You ___ study and help people.
3 People ___ cheat.
4 You ___ be noisy in class.

a Which verb do we use for rules and strong obligations?
b Which verb do we use for advice?
c Which verb means you are not allowed to?
d Do we use *to* after *must*, *may not*, and *should*?
e Do we add an *-s* in the third person singular forms of *must*, *may not*, and *should*?

More practice ⇨ Workbook page 41

5 **Choose the correct words.**

1 Children **must** / **should** go to elementary school.
2 You're tired. You **must** / **should** go to bed.
3 Students **may not** / **shouldn't** eat in class.
4 We **may not** / **shouldn't** go out. It's raining.
5 You **must** / **should** be over eighteen to vote.
6 You're cold. You **must** / **should** wear a coat.

6 **ACTIVATE Work in groups. Write rules and advice for the places in the box using *must* / *may not* and *should* / *shouldn't*. Then compare your ideas with another group.**

cafeteria library classroom
halls schoolyard gym

Students may not shout in the cafeteria.

You shouldn't run in the halls.

Finished?
Write sentences about life with your family using *should*, *must*, and *may not*.

READING ■ Cheating

I can give my opinions about cheating at school.

1 Which of these things are cheating? Read the text and check the things that are mentioned.

1 Copying someone's answers on a test.
2 Copying someone's homework.
3 Doing homework with a friend.
4 E-mailing test questions to a friend.
5 Copying an essay on the Internet.
6 Getting information on the Internet.
7 Writing an essay for someone.
8 Using a calculator on a test.

2 2.20 **Read the text again and complete gaps 1–5 with sentences a–f. There is one sentence that you do not need. Then listen to the text and check your answers.**

a There is more competition today.
b Many students don't even realize that what they're doing is wrong.
c School principals can suspend or expel students who cheat.
d That's a lot of cheaters!
e But it isn't only at school that people are cheating.
f You can pay people online to write an essay for you.

3 BUILD YOUR VOCABULARY Find the British English words in the text.

American English	British English
high school	*secondary school*
smart	1___
grades	2___
cell phones	3___

4 Match the British English words in the box with the American English words in 1–10.

shop biscuit trousers sweet lorry motorway petrol film rubbish pavement

1 gasoline ___
2 movie ___
3 trash ___
4 freeway ___
5 store ___
6 pants ___
7 cookie ___
8 sidewalk ___
9 truck ___
10 candy ___

5 Study the key phrases. Which phrases can you use to disagree with an opinion?

KEY PHRASES ○ Agreeing and disagreeing

I (don't) think that ... .
I agree / disagree with that / you.
That's right.
I (don't) think so.
I'm not sure about that.
Yes, I think you're right.
That's true, but ... .

6 YOUR OPINIONS Ask and answer the questions. Use the key phrases and your own ideas.

1 Do you have to cheat sometimes if you want to succeed?
2 Is it easy to cheat nowadays?
3 What should schools do with cheaters?
4 Are you really cheating if you copy someone's homework?
5 Should schools ask students to report people who cheat?

CHEAT!

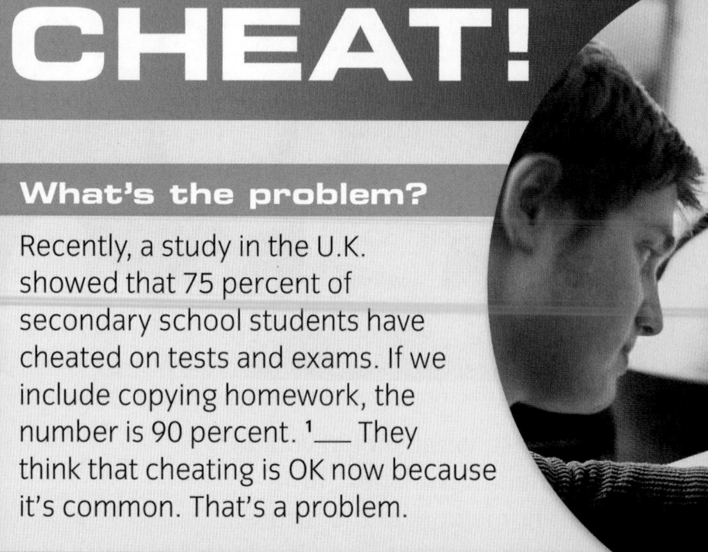

What's the problem?

Recently, a study in the U.K. showed that 75 percent of secondary school students have cheated on tests and exams. If we include copying homework, the number is 90 percent. 1___ They think that cheating is OK now because it's common. That's a problem.

Who's cheating?

In the past, weaker students cheated, but now cheaters are often clever kids who need higher marks. 2___ One secondary school student says, "There's big pressure to get into a good university. You have to get good marks, and to get good marks, some people think they have to cheat."

LANGUAGE FOCUS ■ *have to* and *don't have to*

I can talk about rules at home and at school.

1 **Complete the sentences from the text. Then choose the correct words in the rules. How do we form questions with *have to*?**

1 You ___ get good marks.
2 People sometimes ___ lie and cheat to succeed.
3 ... they ___ cheat to be successful.

RULES

1 We use **have to** / **don't have to** to express an obligation.
2 We use **have to** / **don't have to** when there is no obligation.

More practice ⇨ Workbook page 41

2 **Order the words to make questions.**

1 we / walk / to / school / have to / do
2 plan / classes / the teacher / does / have to
3 they / uniform / wear / have to / don't / a
4 doesn't / Francis / study / have to
5 see / have to / he / the / principal / does
6 have to / you / go / home / do

3 2.21 **Listen to an interview with Natalie. Check the things she has to do. Then write sentences with *have to* and *don't have to*.**

get up early on school days
Natalie doesn't have to get up early on school days.

1 walk to school
2 wear a uniform
3 eat at the cafeteria
4 do her homework before she goes out
5 help make dinner every evening
6 stay home on school days

4 ACTIVATE **Write six questions with *have to*, the words in the boxes, and your own ideas. Then interview your partner.**

parents teacher you friends

cook at home get up at six o'clock do homework on the weekend study English take tests

Do your parents have to get up at six o'clock?

My mom has to get up at six because she starts work early, but my dad doesn't. He doesn't have to get up until seven thirty.

Finished?
Write sentences about an ideal school.
In my ideal school, we only have to go to school for four hours a day. We don't have to ... .

The culture of cheating

In the British study, 50 percent of students agreed with the opinion "People sometimes have to lie and cheat to succeed." It seems that cheating has become normal for some people. [3]___ We see more and more cheaters in sports and in business. Unfortunately, adults don't always set a good example.

How are they cheating?

Cheating is easier with new technology. There are websites where you can download tests and essays. [4]___ Students are instant messaging homework answers and they can send text messages to friends in tests or put answers into their MP3 players. Some students take pictures of tests and then e-mail them to friends.
So, what's the solution?

Beating the cheaters

Teachers can ban mobile phones and cameras, and use special software to detect copying in homework. [5]___ But really it's more important for people to know that they don't have to cheat to be successful – cheaters never win and winners never cheat.

VOCABULARY AND LISTENING ■ School life: nouns

I can understand people talking about schools.

1 **Complete the table with the words in blue. Then answer the questions with a partner.**

Types of school	Other collocations
coed schools	*school leaving age*

1 Which are better: coed schools or single-sex schools, public schools or private schools?
2 What's the best school leaving age? Why?
3 Are school uniforms and school rules a good idea?
4 Are school vacations too long or too short?
5 Which are the most useful school subjects?
6 Should elementary, middle, and high schools be combined?
7 Why are boarding schools necessary?
8 What is the school leaving age and what college entrance exams do students take?

2 2.22 **Listen to four people. Which type of school from exercise 1 does each person go to?**

3 2.23 **Look at the pictures. Are sentences 1–3 *true* or *false*? Listen and check.**

1 Juliet's parents don't have to teach her.
2 Larry thinks that single-sex schools are better.
3 Boys at Wayne's school may not wear their hair too long.

4 2.23 **Listen again and choose the correct answers.**

1 Juliet studies at home because her parents ...
 a are both tutors. b prefer homeschooling.
 c didn't want her to go to the local school.
2 What does Larry dislike about his school?
 a There are no girls. b There are strict rules.
 c He has to wear a uniform.
3 Larry thinks that classes should be coed because ...
 a students are happier in coed classes.
 b girls and boys are together in real life.
 c test scores are better in coed schools.
4 Wayne must study ... because he hasn't cut his hair.
 a at home. b with other students.
 c alone in a different room.
5 Which student is very happy with his / her type of education?
 a Larry b Wayne c Juliet

5 ACTIVATE **Work in groups. Write one good thing and one bad thing about 1–6. Then exchange opinions with another group.**

The bad thing about private schools is that you have to pay.

1 private schools
2 boarding schools
3 single-sex schools
4 school vacations
5 school uniforms
6 homeschooling

SCHOOLS: WHAT'S BEST?

Homeschooling: Juliet studies at home with a tutor.

Single-sex schools: Larry is at an all-boys' school.

School uniforms and appearance: At Wayne's school, the rules about hair are very clear.

I can compare my school to schools in other countries.

1 **Complete the sentences from the listening on page 52 with the words in the box.**

has to   should   don't have to   may not   ~~shouldn't~~   must study   have to

Recommendation

Schools *shouldn't* have separate classes for boys and girls.
Boys and girls [1]___ be in the same class.

Obligation

The school [2]___ take Wayne back because he isn't sixteen.
We [3]___ wear the same uniform.
He [4]___ in a different room from other students.
Boys [5]___ have hair to their shoulders.

No obligation

They [6]___ teach me.

More practice ⇨ Workbook page 43

2 2.24 **Read the text and choose the correct words. Then listen and check your answers.**

School rules

he U.K.

he school leaving age in the U.K. is sixteen, but you **nay not / don't have to** leave school at sixteen.

he U.S.

tudents in many American schools [2]**may not / should** ave chewing gum. It's against the rules. In some states ke Florida, students [3]**must / should** stay at school until ney are eighteen. It's the legal school leaving age. In ther states, like Iowa, they [4]**may not / don't have to** go o school after the age of sixteen. Some people think that ll states [5]**should / have to** change the school leaving ge to eighteen because sixteen is too young.

apan

hildren [6]**have to / should** pass a test before they can o to some elementary schools. Some high schools say vhich movies students [7]**may not / don't have to** watch t the movie theater. Some students think the school **shouldn't / has to** do this because the movie theater sn't at school.

hailand

n Thailand, students [9]**must / may not** clean their lassrooms. They also [10]**have to / shouldn't** sing the ational anthem before school.

3 **Write true sentences using *have to, don't have to,* and *may not.***

I / wear / a school uniform
I don't have to wear a school uniform.

1 I / walk to school
2 parents / get up at 6 a.m.
3 best friend / leave home early
4 students / eat in the classroom
5 I / learn Spanish
6 friends and I / help at home
7 mom / drive to work
8 we / run in the halls

4 **Complete the sentences with your own ideas about school. Then compare with a partner.**

1 The school leaving age should ___.
2 In an ideal school, students don't have to ___.
3 We have to study ___.
4 Our rules say that people may not ___.
5 Teachers shouldn't ___.
6 At lunchtime, students must ___.

STUDY STRATEGY ■ Improving your English

5 **Work in pairs. Think of ways to improve your English, both in and out of school. Write sentences.**

I shouldn't talk in class.
I must try to watch some DVDs in English.

6 ACTIVATE **Work in pairs. Write sentences about your school with *should(n't), must, may not,* or *(don't) have to.* Use the ideas in the box and your own ideas. Then compare your school with the schools in exercise 2.**

stand up when the teacher enters the class
chew gum   leave school at sixteen
wear a uniform   clean the classroom
eat at school   sing the national anthem

We may not chew gum in class.
We don't have to leave school at sixteen.

Pronunciation: Weak forms ⇨ Workbook page 91

Finished?

Write about your school and school life. What is good and bad about it?

I go to the local school. It's a coed school like all public schools. A good thing about my school is that it ... .

SPEAKING ■ Asking for and giving advice

I can ask for and give advice.

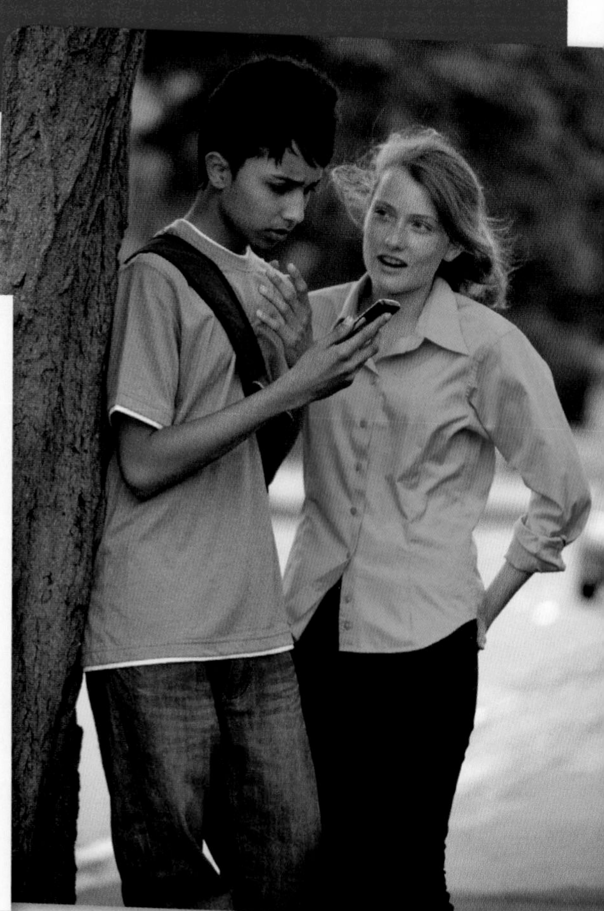

1 **Look at the picture. What is Adam doing?**

2 2.25 **Listen to the dialogue. What three things does Lucy advise?**

Lucy	You look upset, Adam. What's the matter?
Adam	Nothing. I don't want to talk about it.
Lucy	Come on. What's up?
Adam	Well, I just got this text message from a guy in my class. He wants me to take a picture of the math test tomorrow and then send it to him. What should I do, Lucy?
Lucy	Well, whatever you do, don't cheat. That's for sure. They can expel you for that.
Adam	Right.
Lucy	And I think you should tell your teacher.
Adam	What? Tell on him? I can't do that!
Lucy	OK, but you should tell him you won't do it.
Adam	Are you sure?
Lucy	Yes, definitely. Don't worry. I'm sure he'll understand.
Adam	Yes, you're right. Thanks, Lucy.

3 2.26 **Complete the key phrases from the dialogue. Then listen and check. Practice the dialogue with a partner.**

KEY PHRASES ○ Asking for and giving advice

What's the [1]___?
What [2]___ I do?
Whatever you [3]___, don't ... .
That's [4]___ sure.
I think [5]___ should ... .
Are you [6]___?

4 **Match sentences 1–6 with responses a–g. There is one response that you do not need.**

1 What's the matter?
2 What should I do?
3 Are you sure?
4 I think you should tell your parents.
5 Whatever you do, don't forget.
6 Can I copy your homework, Amy?

a No, that's cheating.
b You should tell someone.
c What? I can't do that!
d I don't want to talk about it.
e OK, I won't.
f Don't worry.
g Yes, definitely.

5 2.27 **Listen to the sentences. Which word or words are stressed in each sentence?**

1 What's the matter?
2 I don't want to talk about it.
3 What should I do?
4 Whatever you do, don't answer it.
5 I think you should show it to your teacher.

6 **Work in pairs. Give advice for each situation.**

I just failed my English test.

I think you should study more next time.

1 My brother is always truant.
2 My friend isn't talking to me.
3 The principal has suspended me because of my clothes.
4 I don't understand this homework.
5 A girl in my class has sent me a nasty e-mail.
6 A friend has sent me a picture of tomorrow's test.

7 **ACTIVATE** **Prepare a new dialogue with a partner. Use one of the situations in exercise 6 or your own ideas. Practice your dialogue. Then change roles.**

WRITING ■ An opinion essay

I can write an opinion essay.

5

Are you in favor of school uniforms or against them? Should your school change its policy?

1 At most schools in our area, people don't have to wear a school uniform, but at our school it's compulsory. There is a debate right now about changing this policy. A lot of students are against school uniforms because they like to choose their own clothes. Our uniform isn't great, but I'm in favor of the policy.

2 In my opinion, school uniforms are good for several reasons. Firstly, there isn't any clothes "competition" at school. We all wear the same thing and you don't feel good or bad about your clothes. Secondly, I don't have to think about what to wear every morning. It's very convenient. Also, it is cheaper for families if students wear uniforms because they don't have to buy so many different clothes. Finally, I like to look different when I'm out of school.

3 All in all, I think that it's a good thing to have a school uniform and for that reason, I don't think that the school's policy should change.

1 **Read the model text and answer the questions.**

1 How many arguments does the writer give in favor of school uniforms?
2 Which paragraph summarizes the writer's opinion?
3 How is the writer's school different from most schools in the same area?
4 Why are students against school uniforms?
5 Which opinions do you agree with?

2 **Study the key phrases. Which two phrases can you use in the conclusion of an opinion essay?**

KEY PHRASES ○ Expressing opinions

I'm (not) in favor of … .
I'm against … .
In my opinion / view, … for two / several / various reasons.
All in all, … . / In conclusion, … .
I think that it's a good / bad thing to … .

Language point: Ordering information

3 **Look at sentences a–f and choose the four best reasons for learning English. Then write a paragraph using the linkers in the box.**

Learning English is important for several reasons. Firstly, …

Firstly	Secondly	Also	Finally

a It's an interesting language.
b I want to travel.
c I want to understand pop songs in English.
d It's useful if you want to get a job in the U.S.
e I want to talk to people from other countries.
f It's useful when you use the Internet.

4 **ACTIVATE** **Follow the steps in the writing guide.**

○ WRITING GUIDE

A TASK

Write an opinion essay on this topic: *Are you in favor of boarding schools or against them?*

B THINK AND PLAN

1 Do you know anyone who goes to a boarding school?
2 Are boarding schools common?
3 What do you think of them?
4 Write either three / four points in favor of boarding schools or three / four points against them.
5 Are boarding schools better for some people than for others?

C WRITE

Paragraph 1: Introduction
In our area, …
Paragraph 2: Your opinion
In my opinion, …
Paragraph 3: Conclusion
All in all, …

D CHECK

- paragraphs
- ordering information
- *should, must, have to*

Vocabulary

1 Complete the phrases with the verbs in the box.

suspend make cheat copy bully
get pass leave

1 ___ young students
2 ___ on a test
3 ___ a test
4 ___ a friend's work
5 ___ school at eighteen
6 ___ new friends
7 ___ bad grades
8 ___ a student for being truant

2 Match the words in the box with the definitions.

high school boarding school
elementary school public school
school rules school uniform coed school
single-sex school

1 Special clothes you must wear to school.
2 School for children from 4 to 11 years old.
3 School for children over 14 years old.
4 Students live at this school.
5 Boys and girls go to this school.
6 Only girls go to this school.
7 Students must follow these.
8 You don't pay for this school.

Language focus

3 Write true sentences with *have to*.

1 I / make dinner
2 parents / get up at 7 a.m.
3 best friend / leave home early
4 dad / drive to work
5 I / learn French
6 friends and I / help at home
7 I / wear a school uniform
8 our teacher / correct our tests

4 Write questions for the sentences in exercise 3. Then write true short answers.

Do you have to wear a school uniform?
No, I don't.

5 Choose the correct words.

1 You **may not** / **shouldn't** leave your motorcycle there. It isn't safe.
2 He's lucky because he **may not** / **doesn't have to** wear a school uniform.
3 We **may not** / **don't have to** use cell phones. It's against the rules.
4 I **have to** / **should** walk to school because there isn't a bus.
5 Young people **must** / **should** go to school until the age of eighteen. It's the law.
6 You **may not** / **don't have to** cheat on tests.

Communication

6 Choose the correct answers.

1 What should I do?
a That's for sure. b Yes, definitely.
c Whatever you do, don't worry.
2 I got a bad grade on my math test.
a Right. b Oh, come on!
c You should work harder.
3 What's the matter?
a That's right. b Nothing.
c Are you OK?
4 You should tell your parents.
a Are you sure? b What's up?
c What should I do?
5 People should stay at school until they are 18.
a I'm OK. b I agree with you.
c Are you sure?
6 Do you think that school uniforms are good?
a Yes, you're right. b I don't agree.
c They're OK.

Listening

7 2.28 Listen to four people talking about school. Match speakers 1–4 with sentences a–e. There is one sentence that you do not need.

Speaker 1 ___ Speaker 3 ___
Speaker 2 ___ Speaker 4 ___

a The school leaving age should be sixteen all over the U.S.
b Our high school isn't very good.
c Schools shouldn't expel students who cheat on tests.
d It's important to tell a teacher about bullying.
e I study at home.

1 Read the survey and questions 1–4. Are your answers the same as the most popular ones?

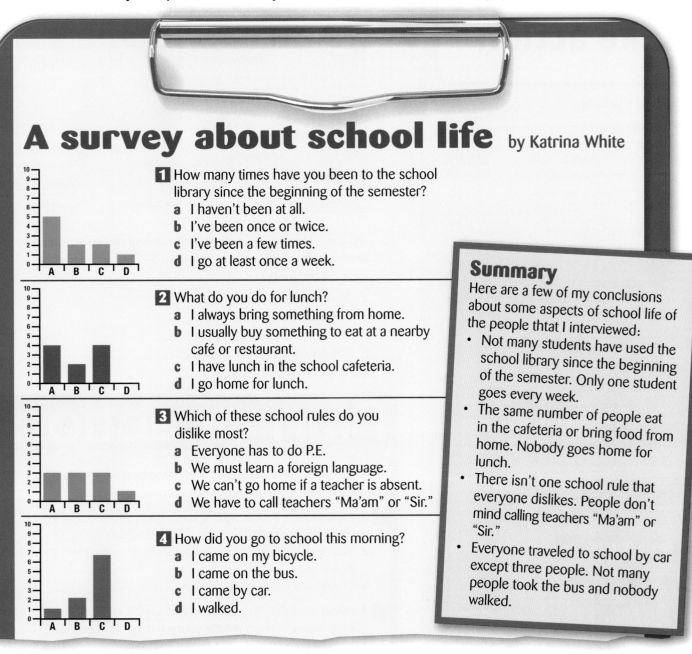

A survey about school life by Katrina White

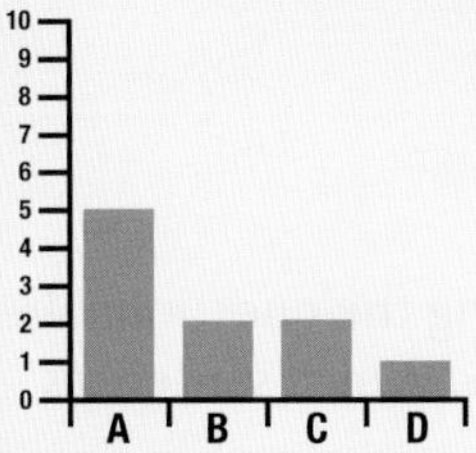

1 How many times have you been to the school library since the beginning of the semester?

- **a** I haven't been at all.
- **b** I've been once or twice.
- **c** I've been a few times.
- **d** I go at least once a week.

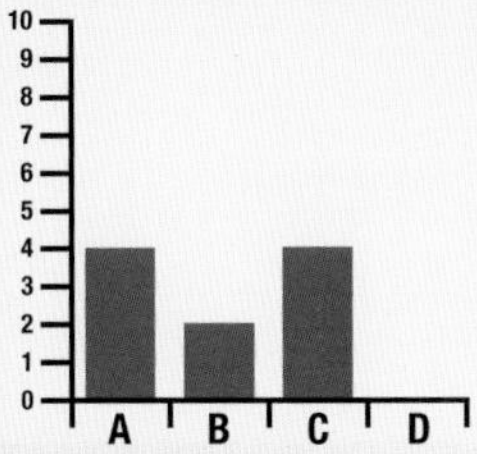

2 What do you do for lunch?

- **a** I always bring something from home.
- **b** I usually buy something to eat at a nearby café or restaurant.
- **c** I have lunch in the school cafeteria.
- **d** I go home for lunch.

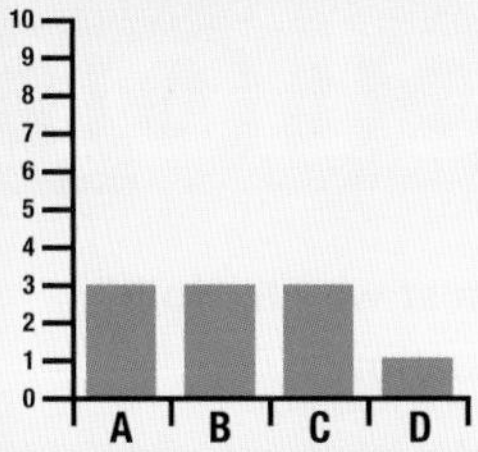

3 Which of these school rules do you dislike most?

- **a** Everyone has to do P.E.
- **b** We must learn a foreign language.
- **c** We can't go home if a teacher is absent.
- **d** We have to call teachers "Ma'am" or "Sir."

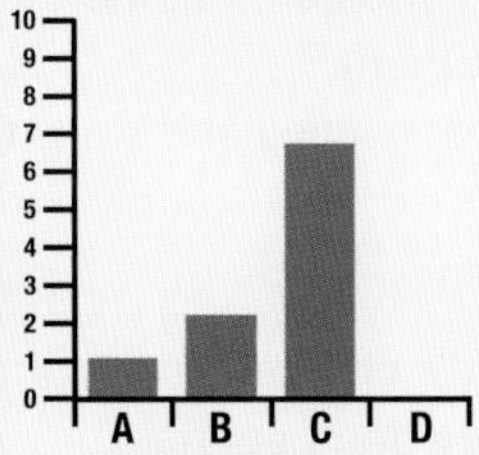

4 How did you go to school this morning?

- **a** I came on my bicycle.
- **b** I came on the bus.
- **c** I came by car.
- **d** I walked.

Summary

Here are a few of my conclusions about some aspects of school life of the people thtat I interviewed:

- Not many students have used the school library since the beginning of the semester. Only one student goes every week.
- The same number of people eat in the cafeteria or bring food from home. Nobody goes home for lunch.
- There isn't one school rule that everyone dislikes. People don't mind calling teachers "Ma'am" or "Sir."
- Everyone traveled to school by car except three people. Not many people took the bus and nobody walked.

2 Write a survey about school life. Follow the steps in the project checklist.

PROJECT CHECKLIST

1. Read questions 1–4 below. Think of four possible answers for each one.
   1. How many times have you used the Internet for school work since the beginning of the semester?
   2. When did you last go on a school trip?
   3. How much homework do you usually get in these subjects: math, English, history, and science?
   4. What classroom rules do you dislike most?
2. Write each question with the four possible answers.
3. Ask ten people the questions and note their answers.
4. Draw charts to represent the results.
5. Write a summary with some conclusions about the results.

3 Exchange your survey with the rest of the class. Who has the most interesting answers and results?

Take action

Start thinking

1 Is there a problem with food waste in your country?
2 What charities are popular in your country?
3 Why is the Amazon rainforest in danger?

Aims

Communication: I can ...

- express certainty and possibility.
- understand a text about food waste.
- speculate about the future.
- understand an interview about rainforests.
- talk about the future.
- make plans and arrangements.
- write a formal letter.

Vocabulary

- Action and protest
- Phrasal verbs: a campaign

Language focus

- *will* and *might*
- First conditional
- *be going to* and *will*
- Present continuous for future arrangements

Reach Out Options

Extra listening and speaking
Interviewing a campaigner
Page 93

Curriculum extra
Geography: Natural environments
Page 101

Culture
Charities: Comic Relief
Page 109

Vocabulary bank
Negative prefixes: *un-*, *im-*, and *in-*; The environment
Page 117

VOCABULARY AND LANGUAGE FOCUS
Action and protest

I can express certainty and possibility.

1 Complete the table with the words in blue in the *Plan of action* questionnaire. Then do the questionnaire.

Verb	Noun	Verb	Noun
publicize	publicity	7 ___	volunteer
meet	1 ___	support	8 ___
2 ___	organization	sponsor	9 ___
march	3 ___	petition	10 ___
4 ___	donation	11 ___	ban
collect	5 ___	12 ___	boycott
protest	6 ___	campaign	13 ___

2 2.33 **Listen to two people discussing the questionnaire. Match opinions a–e with dialogues 1–5. Which sentences express certainty?**

a "It might help a little." ___
b "That definitely won't help." ___
c "It might not be a good idea." ___
d "That will definitely work better." ___
e "It will be more effective." ___

Plan of action

You can change the world, but what's the best way to do it? Choose the best plan of action for each situation.

1 Some buildings in your school are in bad condition, but the government isn't spending any money on them.
 a You need publicity. Invite journalists to a meeting and show them the buildings.
 b Organize a march in the streets.

2 A charity says that 50 percent of the world's children are poor and hungry. Many of them will die young if they don't get help.
 a Donate some money and organize a collection of clothes for the charity.
 b Organize a small protest. The government isn't helping enough.

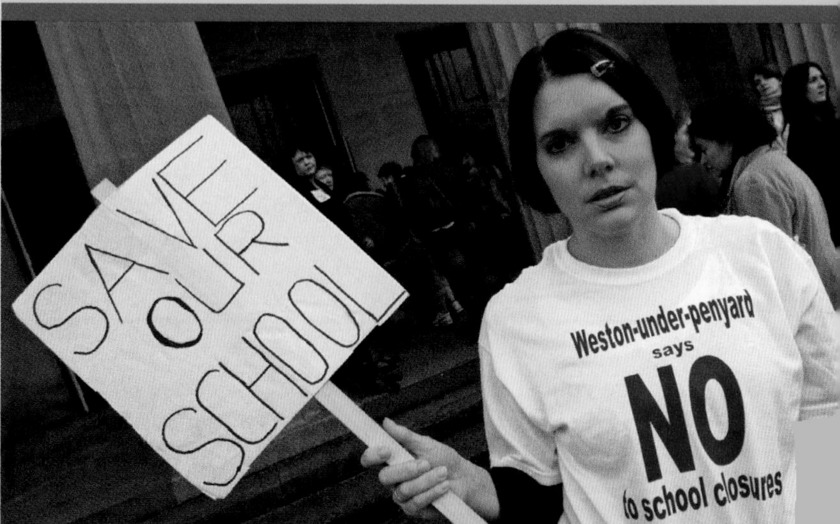

3 **Complete the key phrases with the words in the box. Which phrases make suggestions? Which phrases comment on suggestions?**

help about thing could don't idea think work

KEY PHRASES ◯ Making suggestions

Let's (organize a meeting).
That isn't a bad [1]___.
That should / could / might [2]___ a little.
How [3]___ (starting an e-mail campaign)?
I [4]___ we should try … .
Why [5]___ we (boycott the stores)?
That will definitely [6]___ better.
I think the best [7]___ to do is … .
We [8]___ write to the city council.

4 **Write suggestions for problems 1–4.**

Let's write a letter to the city council and ask for more trash cans.

1 There's a lot of trash in your town.
2 A new law says that students must go to school on Saturdays.
3 Two people from your town want to participate in the Paralympic Games, but they don't have any money.
4 Your local movie theater is closing.

3 Your community needs a new community center, but there isn't enough money for it.
  a Volunteer to help to build the community center.
  b Organize a sports event. Look for supporters and sponsors.

4 Parents are unhappy because some stores in town are selling violent video games to children.
  a Start a petition to ban all violent video games. If a lot of people sign, the council might do something about the problem.
  b Have a meeting with the owners of the stores. They must be stricter about who buys violent games.

5 A chain of big supermarkets isn't paying enough to Chilean farmers who produce fruit for the stores.
  a Boycott those supermarkets and start an e-mail campaign. The supermarkets won't like the bad publicity. It will affect their sales.
  b Collect money for a trip to Chile. Visit the farmers and show your support for them.

will and *might*

5 **Study examples a–d and complete rules 1–4. Then find more examples of *will* and *might* in the questionnaire.**

a I might volunteer if have time.
b This might not work. I'm not sure.
c She's agreed. She'll support us.
d Your plan won't work. It's impossible.

◯ RULES

1 Examples ___ and ___ express certainty about the future.
2 Examples ___ and ___ express possibility about the future.
3 Short forms of *will* / *will not* are ___ and ___.
4 *Will* and *might* ___ change in the third person singular forms.

More practice ⇨ Workbook page 49

6 **Write the sentences using *will*, *won't*, *might*, and *might not*.**

you / see / me tomorrow. (maybe not)
You might not see me tomorrow.

1 Joe / donate / some money (definitely)
2 she / volunteer / to help (maybe)
3 people / listen / to us (maybe not)
4 I / live / here in 2020 (definitely not)
5 the government / change (definitely)
6 the world / be / a better place one day (maybe)

7 **ACTIVATE Work in groups. Talk about the future using the ideas in the boxes.**

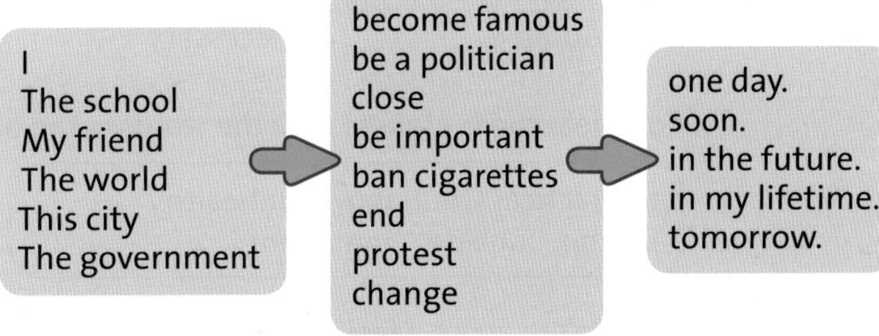

I
The school
My friend
The world
This city
The government
become famous
be a politician
close
be important
ban cigarettes
end
protest
change
one day.
soon.
in the future.
in my lifetime.
tomorrow.

I might become famous one day.

◯ *Finished?*
Think of more ideas about your future. Write sentences with *will*, *won't*, *might*, and *might not*.
I might not get married.

READING ■ The food waste scandal

I can understand a text about food waste.

1 2.34 **Look at the title of the text and the pictures and answer the questions. Then read and listen to the text and check your answers.**

1 What is happening in the pictures?
2 Why do supermarkets throw away so much food?
3 Who are freegans?

2 Read the text again and choose the correct answers.

1 What type of text is it?
 a a supermarket website
 b an educational leaflet
 c a protest group handout
2 The author wrote the text to ...
 a invite. b advertise. c complain.
3 Why do freegans eat food from trash cans?
 a Because they're hungry.
 b To show that it's safe to eat it.
 c To protest against food waste.
4 How much food never gets to supermarkets?
 a Forty percent of all food in the world.
 b Six million tons of food.
 c One third of food supplies.
5 Which protest action does the text not suggest?
 a A supermarket boycott. b A petition.
 c A public protest.
6 The text encourages people to ...
 a support freegans.
 b stop buying papayas.
 c give food to the poor.

3 BUILD YOUR VOCABULARY Find the opposites of words 1–4 in the text.

1 perfect 3 sensitive
2 acceptable 4 necessary

4 Complete the sentences with the words in the box.

impractical	unhappy	unhealthy
insane	unkind	impatient

1 I don't exercise. I feel very ___.
2 I like you, and I'll be ___ when you go.
3 Why are you talking to your backpack? That's ___!
4 We can't organize a protest in one day. It's ___.
5 Why are some people ___ to animals?
6 We can't change society in a week. You're too ___!

5 YOUR OPINIONS Ask and answer the questions.

1 What actions against supermarkets does the text suggest? Do you think they are likely to be effective?
2 Which piece of information in the text shocks you most?
3 Could you be a freegan? Why / Why not?
4 How much food do your family and friends throw away? Why?
5 How do you feel about eating fruit and vegetables that are not perfect? Why?

Freegans against supermarket waste

It is World Food Day on October 16, so the local freegan group is organizing protest actions against food waste.

Who are we?

We, freegans, believe that it is wrong to throw food away when millions of people are hungry. We get most of our food from supermarket trash cans and dumpsters because we want to draw attention to this unacceptable food waste scandal.

The facts

Over one third of all world food supplies ends up as waste and much of this waste occurs before food reaches the stores. Supermarkets can force farmers to throw away up to 40 percent of their crops if they are imperfect – not all the same size or not looking nice. A U.S. survey has shown that each year our supermarkets waste over 33 million tons of food and a lot of it is perfectly safe to eat, including:

- 8 percent of the fresh fruit and vegetables
- 28 percent of the veal
- 51 percent of the papayas

1 **Complete the first conditional sentences from the text. When do we use a comma in these sentences?**

Situation	Result
If we all [1] ___ the supermarkets,	they [2] ___ to us.
If everyone signs the petition,	will it make a difference?

Result	Situation
Supermarkets [3] ___	if only a few people [4] ___.
What will the supermarkets do	if we organize a huge protest march?

More practice ⇨ Workbook page 49

What we want

We aren't against supermarkets; we just want them to change their insensitive attitude and reduce all this unnecessary waste. They should:

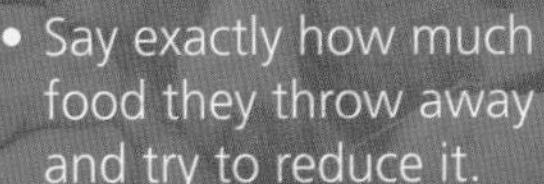

- Say exactly how much food they throw away and try to reduce it.
- Give the food to charities which distribute it to poor people.
- Sell fruit and vegetables that don't look perfect.

What you can do

Supermarkets won't change if only a few people protest. If we all boycott the supermarkets, they'll listen to us. You'll find more information and an online petition if you look on our website.

We need support for our campaign. Become a volunteer or just spread the word. Come to the public meeting and share your ideas!

2 **Study the sentences in exercise 1 and complete the rules. Use *will, won't,* and *the simple present.***

RULES

1. We use the first conditional to talk about a likely or possible future situation and to describe its result.
2. We talk about the likely or possible future situation with *if* + ___.
3. We describe the result with ___ or ___ + base form.

3 **Complete the sentences with the first conditional form of the verbs in parentheses.**

1. If he (support) us, we (win).
2. If we (ask) people, a lot of them (volunteer).
3. She (boycott) the store if it (sell) violent video games.
4. People (not know) about it if we (not organize) a meeting.
5. If you (ban) cars from downtown, the store owners (not be) happy.
6. I (not sponsor) you if you (not finish) the race.

4 **Complete the sentences with your own ideas.**

If I don't pass this test, ***I'll have to do it again.***

1. If I don't finish my homework, ___.
2. If I stay in this evening, ___.
3. If it rains tomorrow, ___.
4. If my favorite actor comes to town, ___.
5. If I don't go on vacation, ___.
6. If you help me with my math, ___.
7. If my friend isn't at school, ___.
8. If my mother doesn't feel well, ___.

5 ACTIVATE **Work in pairs. Ask and answer questions about the future. Use the sentences in exercise 4 or your own ideas.**

What will you do if you stay in this evening?

I'll have to help my mom with dinner.

Pronunciation: Linking ⇨ Workbook page 91

Finished?

Continue the chain of consequences.

If I go camping this weekend, I won't study for my tests. If I don't study for my tests, I ... .

VOCABULARY AND LISTENING ■ Phrasal verbs: a campaign

I can understand an interview about rainforests.

1 2.35 **Read and listen to the text and check the meaning of the verbs in blue. Then match the verbs with synonyms 1–8.**

1 finish
2 start
3 continue
4 care for
5 discover
6 destroy
7 participate in
8 subscribe to

The world's rainforests are in danger and we must look after them. When we destroy forests, we wipe out plant and animal species. If we carry on the destruction, we'll end up in a sadder, grayer world. The future won't be bright. Our children and grandchildren will blame us for doing nothing. I'm going to set up a campaign so people can find out how they can help. To publicize my campaign, I'm going to visit the Amazon rainforest next July, where I'm going to swim a hundred kilometers in the Amazon River in ten days. You can sign up for my newsletter and join in the activities on my website, or watch the documentary on TV.

Molly Osborne

STUDY STRATEGY ○ Making your own examples

2 Complete the sentences with your own examples. Then compare with a partner and try to memorize the best sentences.

1 I want to set up a club for ___.
2 If you carry on shouting, I'll ___.
3 We're ___. Do you want to join in?
4 Before I'm old, I want to find out ___.
5 I think that ___ might wipe out humans.
6 If you smoke, you're going to end up ___.
7 I think we should look after ___.
8 Sign up for my newsletter and you'll get a free ___.

3 2.36 **A journalist is interviewing Molly Osborne. Which two questions do you think are not in the interview? Listen and check your answers.**

1 What's your campaign about?
2 How much money will you make from sponsors?
3 Are you going to steal some of the money?
4 What problems do you think you'll have?
5 Will you keep going if there are piranhas in the river?
6 Is someone going to look after you while you're there?
7 How many cars are you going to buy?
8 When's the documentary going to be on TV?

4 2.36 **Listen again. What are Molly's answers to the questions in exercise 3?**

5 ACTIVATE **Work in groups. Look at the information. You are organizing a campaign to help save whales. Make suggestions about the ideas in the box using the key phrases on page 59. Think about where, when, and how to organize these things. Then exchange opinions with another group.**

campaign | set up a petition | protest march | sponsored sports event | create a website | write a newsletter | prepare leaflets

Many species of whales are disappearing from our oceans. Humans are killing them for meat and some of it is used to make pet food! If we don't do something now, we will wipe out these magnificent animals forever.

LANGUAGE FOCUS ■ *be going to* and *will*

I can talk about the future.

6

Plans and predictions

1 **Complete the sentences from the text and exercise 3 on page 62. Then match a–f with rules 1 and 2.**

a Our children ___ blame us for doing nothing.
b The future ___ be bright.
c I ___ swim a hundred kilometers.
d ___ someone ___ look after you?
e What problems do you think you ___ have?
f How much money ___ you make from sponsors?

RULES

1 We use *be going to* to talk about plans.
2 We use *will* / *won't* to make predictions.

More practice ⇨ Workbook page 51

2 **Complete the text with *be going to* or *will* / *won't*.**

Tim and I [1]___ (run) the New York Marathon for charity next month. We hope that all our friends [2]___ (sponsor) us, so we [3]___ (make) a lot of money.

I think that the biggest problem [4]___ (be) getting in shape. That's why we [5]___ (start) training soon. Tim says he [6]___ (run) 10 kilometers before school every day. But I don't think he [7]___ (train) every day because he hates getting up early.

3 **Read the situation. Then complete the questions and invent answers with *be going to* or *will*.**

Situation:
There are plans to close a park and to build office buildings on the land. You want to organize a protest and a free concert for publicity.

1 When ___ the park ___ close?
2 How many office buildings ___ they ___ build?
3 How many people do you think ___ come to the concert?
4 Which groups ___ you ___ invite?
5 What problems do you think you ___ have?
6 How much money do you think the concert ___ raise?

Intentions and instant decisions

4 **Read the dialogue. Then choose the correct words in the rules.**

Anna Hi, Tim. I'm going to run this morning. Are you going to come with me?
Tim I'll join you later.
Anna I'm not going to wait all morning.
Tim Oh, all right, I'll come.

RULES

1 We use ***will*** / ***be going to*** for intentions.
2 We use ***will*** / ***be going to*** for instant decisions.

More practice ⇨ Workbook page 51

5 2.37 **Choose the correct words. Then listen and check.**

Sam [1]**I'm going to** / **I'll** get tickets for the concert today. Do you have one?
Amy No, not yet. [2]**Are you going to** / **Will you** get one for me?
Sam OK, [3]**I'm going to** / **I'll** give it to you at school tomorrow.
Amy Great! Here, [4]**I'm going to** / **I'll** give you the money. How [5]**are you going to** / **will you** get to the concert?
Sam I don't know.
Amy I know. [6]**I'm going to** / **I'll** ask my dad to drive us.
Sam That's a good idea. Thanks, Amy.

6 ACTIVATE **Work in pairs and make dialogues using 1–6. Then continue the dialogues with your own ideas.**

visit Helen in the hospital / come with you

I'm going to visit Helen in the hospital.

I'll come with you. I'll bring her some magazines.

1 see a movie at the mall / come with you
2 go grocery shopping / give you a list
3 have a picnic / make sandwiches
4 do a walk for charity / support you
5 take the dog for a walk / get lunch ready
6 organize a party / help you

Finished?
Invent more situations similar to those in exercise 6.

SPEAKING ■ Plans and arrangements

I can make plans and arrangements.

1 Look at the picture. Adam is going to run for charity. What is he asking the man? Why?

2 2.38 Listen to the dialogue. How much money does Adam think he'll raise?

Adam	Hi, Mr. Johnson. Do you have a minute?
Mr. Johnson	Hello, Adam. What can I do for you?
Adam	I'm doing a ten-kilometer run for charity next month and I'm looking for sponsors.
Mr. Johnson	That's very good, Adam. What's it for?
Adam	It's for a children's charity.
Mr. Johnson	Ten kilometers is quite a distance! How are you going to prepare?
Adam	I'm going to run every morning before school. I'll try to run a little further every day.
Mr. Johnson	And when are you running? What date?
Adam	I'm running on Sunday, May 14. I hope to raise about $150. Will you sponsor me?
Mr. Johnson	Yes, OK. It sounds like a good cause. I hope you finish it!
Adam	I'm going to try! I hope I'll be in shape by then. Some friends are going to do it, too.
Mr. Johnson	Good luck, Adam.
Adam	Thanks.

3 2.39 Complete the key phrases from the dialogue. Who says them? Listen and check your answers. Then practice the dialogue with a partner.

KEY PHRASES ○ Donating money

Do you have a [1]___?
What can I [2]___ for you?
What's it [3]___?
It's [4]___ (a children's charity).
I hope [5]___ about ($150).
It sounds [6]___ a good cause.

Language point: Present continuous for future arrangements

4 Read the rule. Which structures are in sentences a and b?

○ RULE

We can use *be going to* to express plans, but we can also use the present continuous when we talk about arrangements with a fixed date or time in the future.

a I'm running next Sunday.
b Some friends are going to do it, too.

More practice ⇨ Workbook page 51

5 Complete the planner with your own entries for next weekend. Then ask and answer with a partner.

	Saturday	Sunday
Morning	*go to the mall*	
Afternoon	*play basketball*	
Evening		

What are you doing on Saturday morning?

I'm going to the mall.

6 ACTIVATE Prepare a new dialogue with a partner. Use situation 1. Practice your dialogue. Then change roles and use situation 2.

Situation 1
- five-hour basketball marathon
- The Red Cross
- playing next weekend
- target: $350

Situation 2
- three-legged soccer game
- Save the Children
- playing next Saturday
- target: $600

WRITING ■ A formal letter

I can write a formal letter.

6

1 **Read the model text. What is the purpose of the letter? Match paragraphs 1–3 with topics a–d. There is one topic that you do not need.**

a explanation
b invitation
c intentions
d reason for writing

2 **Answer the questions.**

1 What is the name and address of the person who wrote the letter?
2 What is the address of the organization receiving it?
3 How does the main part of the letter start and finish?
4 What is the group going to protest against?

Students Against Nuclear Energy
1549 Black Street
Asheville, NC 28821
April 30, 2013

Morrisey's Supermarket
1444 Carter Avenue
Asheville, NC 28021

Dear Sir or Madam,

1 I represent a group called *Students Against Nuclear Energy*. I am writing to you because we are concerned about plans to build a nuclear power station in our area.

2 In our opinion, nuclear power stations are not safe, so if there is one near our town, the residents might be in danger. If we have a nuclear power station here, it will be a problem for hundreds of years. Renewable energy, on the other hand, is a better alternative as it is cleaner and safer.

3 We have therefore decided to take action and we are going to organize a protest. For this reason, we are sending you a poster and we hope that you will support us and help to publicize this event.

Sincerely,

James West

Group Coordinator

Students Against Nuclear Energy

3 **Match the key phrases with the three correct paragraph topics in exercise 1.**

KEY PHRASES ○ Formal letters

1 In our opinion, ...
2 I represent ... .
3 For this reason, ...
4 On the other hand, ...
5 We have therefore decided to ... .

Language point: Explaining

4 **Find these words in the model text. Then complete sentences 1–4 with your own ideas.**

because as therefore for this reason

1 We are protesting because ___.
2 I am against food waste as ___.
3 The rainforests are in danger. We have therefore decided to ___.
4 I think that circuses are cruel. For this reason, ___.

5 **ACTIVATE Follow the steps in the writing guide.**

○ WRITING GUIDE

A TASK

Your local city council is going to close a park near your town to build a freeway. You want to stop this. Write a letter to the local newspaper.

B THINK AND PLAN

1 What's the name of your organization?
2 Why are you concerned?
3 What problems might a freeway cause?
4 Why is a park better?
5 How are you going to protest?

C WRITE

Paragraph 1: Introduction
I represent a group called ...
Paragraph 2: The problem
In our opinion, ...
Paragraph 3: Action
We have therefore decided to ...

D CHECK

- layout of the letter
- explanation words
- *will* and *be going to*

Vocabulary

1 Write nouns from these verbs.

1 meet ___
2 donate ___
3 campaign ___
4 organize ___
5 collect ___
6 ban ___
7 publicize ___
8 support ___

2 Complete the text with the verbs in the box.

join in | wipe out | sign up | carry on | look after | find out

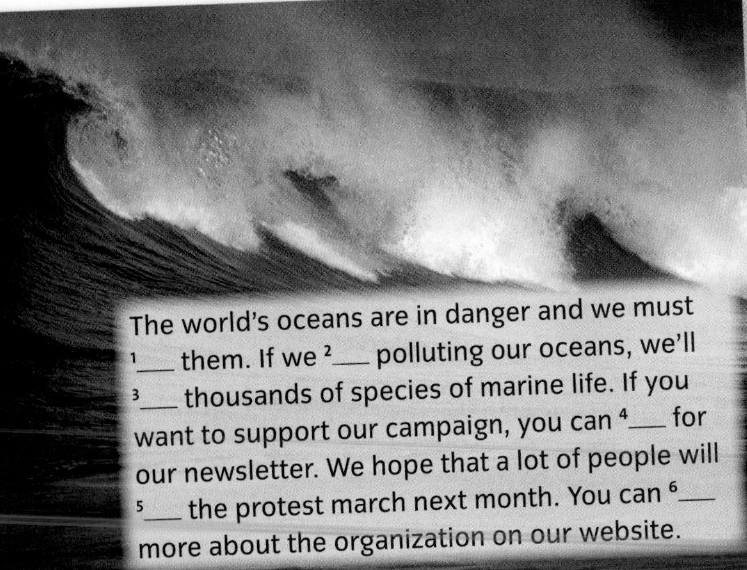

The world's oceans are in danger and we must 1___ them. If we 2___ polluting our oceans, we'll 3___ thousands of species of marine life. If you want to support our campaign, you can 4___ for our newsletter. We hope that a lot of people will 5___ the protest march next month. You can 6___ more about the organization on our website.

3 Write the opposites of these adjectives with *un-*, *im-*, or *in-*.

1 ___happy
2 ___sensitive
3 ___healthy
4 ___practical
5 ___necessary
6 ___acceptable
7 ___possible
8 ___natural

Language focus

4 Complete the sentences with *might*, *be going to*, or *will*.

1 If you don't come now, we ___ definitely miss the train.
2 I ___ join you later. I'm not sure yet.
3 We ___ see a movie tonight. You should come!
4 She ___ sign the petition, but I'm not certain.
5 Do you think a lot of things ___ be better in the future?
6 Tom ___ fail his test if he doesn't study.
7 What ___ you ___ do on Saturday?
8 Do you think it ___ rain this afternoon?

5 Complete the dialogue with *be going to* or *will*.

Chris What 1___ you ___ do tonight? Have you decided?
Ellie I 2___ see a soccer game at Springland Stadium.
Chris Cool. I 3___ come with you.
Ellie You don't have a ticket.
Chris No problem! I 4___ buy one at the gate. How 5___ you ___ get there?
Ellie My dad 6___ drive me there.
Chris Do you think he 7___ take me, too?
Ellie No, I'm sorry. There are five of us already.
Chris Never mind. I 8___ get the bus.

Communication

6 Complete the dialogue with the phrases in the box.

might help | much effect | Let's | could | will have to | how about | Why don't | won't help

Allison What are we going to do? The city council wants to close the community center.
Stuart 1___ we organize a protest march?
Allison That's not a bad idea. We 2___ also start a petition.
Stuart That 3___, but we'll need a lot of signatures.
Allison 4___ have a meeting on Saturday.
Stuart OK. I'll send invitations by e-mail.
Allison If a lot of people come, the city council 5___ listen to us.
Stuart I don't know. It might not have 6___.
Allison Well, 7___ boycotting all the soccer games?
Stuart That definitely 8___!

Listening

7 2.40 Listen to the dialogue and write *true* or *false*.

1 Ted is putting up posters for a public meeting.
2 They are planning a protest march against a nuclear power station.
3 Ann thinks that renewable energy is better than nuclear power.
4 A lot of elderly people feel the same way as Ann.
5 Ann doesn't want to join the campaign committee.
6 Ann will get people in her neighborhood to sign the petition.

Listening

1 **Look at the pictures and answer the questions.**

1 What aspects of school life do the pictures show?
2 What problems do you think these students have?
3 What rules do you think the students might disagree with?
4 What could the school do?
5 What are the differences and similarities between these schools and your school?

2 2.41 **Listen to a conversation. Which problem in the pictures do Jasmin, Steve, and Jeff talk about?**

3 2.41 **Listen again and complete the sentences.**

1 They don't serve ___ food in the school cafeteria.
2 Jasmin wants to start a ___ against the food.
3 Steve says that they must first organize a ___.
4 Jeff has ___ for lunch.
5 Jeff suggests organizing a ___ around the school.
6 ___ doesn't have to eat in the cafeteria.
7 ___ thinks they should boycott the cafeteria for a day.
8 They decide to organize a meeting at ___.

Speaking

4 **Work in pairs and prepare a conversation about a problem at your school. Imagine you are planning a protest. Answer the questions.**

1 What is the problem?
2 What are the consequences?
3 How do the students and teachers feel about this problem?
4 What do you want to achieve?
5 What actions could you take?

5 **Have a conversation. Use your ideas in exercise 4 and the chart below to help you. One of you is A and one of you is B. Change roles.**

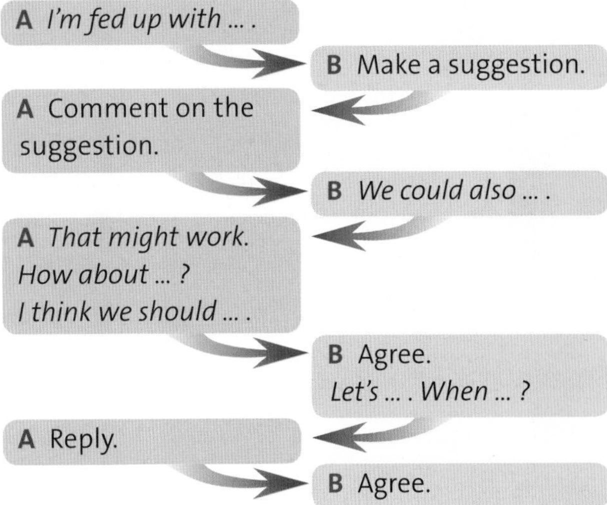

A *I'm fed up with ... .*
B Make a suggestion.
A Comment on the suggestion.
B *We could also ... .*
A *That might work.*
How about ... ?
I think we should ... .
B Agree.
Let's ... . When ... ?
A Reply.
B Agree.

Writing

6 **Write a letter to your principal about a problem. Use the questions in exercise 4 to help you. Explain what the school should do to change things. Say what action the students are going to take. Begin like this:**

Dear Mr. / Mrs. ....,
I represent a group of students ... .

7 Movies and fiction

Start thinking

1 When did the first movie theaters open?
2 What's a blockbuster movie?
3 What kind of book is *The Time Machine*?

Aims

Communication: I can ...

- talk about likes and dislikes.
- understand a text about the history of movie theaters.
- talk about ability and possibility.
- understand a program about books and movies.
- talk about imaginary situations.
- talk about books and movies that I prefer.
- write a book or a movie review.

Vocabulary

- Books and movies: genres
- Books and movies: features

Language focus

- Verbs + *-ing / to*
- *could, can, will be able to*
- Second conditional

Reach Out Options

Extra listening and speaking
Interviewing someone about a movie
Page 94

Curriculum extra
Language and literature: Word building – nouns
Page 102

Culture
The British movie industry
Page 110

Vocabulary bank
Suffixes: *-er* and *-or*; Filmmaking
Page 118

VOCABULARY AND LANGUAGE FOCUS
Books and movies: genres
I can talk about likes and dislikes.

1 Match the words in the boxes with the books and movies 1–8 in the pictures. There are more words than you need.

Nouns
a comedy
a thriller
a drama
a fantasy
a mystery
a musical
a western
a romance
a cartoon

Compound nouns
an adventure
a science fiction
a detective
a war
a horror
a spy
: story / movie

Which book and movie genres suit you best?

1 You've had a long day. What do you enjoy doing most?
a Reading my favorite book.
b Going for a run.
c Watching a DVD with friends.

2 Which best describes your bedroom?
a Messy. There are posters, pictures of friends, and a lot of things everywhere.
b There's a bed, a desk, ... It looks like any other bedroom.
c Pretty neat. Only my desk is a mess.

3 Which quality do you value most?
a imagination **b** intelligence **c** sense of humor

4 Which school subject do you prefer?
a history **b** math **c** languages

5 What job would you like to do?
a I want to do something creative.
b I wouldn't like to do the same job all my life.
c I'd like to work with people.

6 Which statement best describes you?
a I'm a "day dreamer." I enjoy doing unusual things.
b I'm a "get up and go" person. I like being busy.
c I'm a "people person." I hate being alone.

KEY

Mostly a: Mystery and fantasy are your favorite genres. You like reading horror stories and watching science fiction movies. You don't mind watching westerns.

Mostly b: Adventure and drama are your favorite genres. You enjoy reading thrillers and you love watching war movies.

Mostly c: Comedy and romance are your favorite genres. You like reading cartoon stories, but you prefer watching musicals.

2 Invent titles for books and movies using the words and phrases in the boxes. Guess the genre of other people's titles.

The title of the book is Life without Laura.

Is it a romance?

The Man A Woman City Two Kids Songs Battle Voices Life The Story

in of and from with without

Three Brains The Future The Crazy Dogs Laura The Million-Dollar Deal Space The Darkness The Dead A Wedding

3 Do the *Which book and movie genres suit you best?* questionnaire. Then compare your answers with a partner. Do you agree with the key?

1 The Fifth Street Robberies
2 Wedding in Hawaii
3 Zombie Grave
4 Fantasy Land
5 Laughing in the Lab
6 Fame School 3
7 Lost in the Amazon
8 Parallel Universe

Finished?
Write about a book you have read or a movie you have seen recently. Say why you liked / did not like it.
I just read ... . It was ... .

4 Complete the sentences from the questionnaire. What are the negative and short forms of *would*?

Verb	+ *-ing*
I like	***being*** busy.
I hate	[1]___ alone.
You enjoy	[2]___ thrillers.
You [3]___ mind	watching westerns.
Verb	**+ *to***
I [4]___	to do something creative.
I'd like	[5]___ with people.
I [6]___ like	to do the same job all my life.

More practice ⇨ Workbook page 57

5 3.02 Listen. Do these verbs go with *to* or *-ing*?

prefer decide 'd prefer love finish need

6 Complete the sentences about you and people who you know using verbs in exercises 4 and 5 and the phrases in the box.

I like watching DVDs with friends.
My friend would like to be in a musical.

watch DVDs with friends be in a musical read in English live in another country go to Hollywood sing in the shower meet a famous actor or actress

7 ACTIVATE Study the key phrases. Then find out about your partner's likes and dislikes. Ask and answer questions using the key phrases, the ideas in exercise 6, and your own ideas.

KEY PHRASES Expressing likes and dislikes

Would you like to ... ?	Do you like ... ?
Yes, I would.	Yes, I do.
No, I wouldn't.	No, I don't.
I'd love / hate it.	I love / hate it.
I wouldn't mind.	I don't mind.

Do you like watching DVDs with friends?

Yes, I love it.

READING ■ Movie technology

I can understand a text about the history of movie theaters.

1 3.03 **Look at the words in the box and guess the correct order on the timeline. Read and listen to the text and check your answers.**

computer-generated images 3D color digital projectors sound surround sound

Past → Now

1___ 2___ 3___ 4___ 5___ 6___

STUDY STRATEGY ■ Finding specific information

To find specific information, don't read the text in detail. Follow these steps:

1 Identify the key words in the question.
2 Read the text quickly. Look for the key words. Don't stop at difficult words.
3 Read the text around the key words again and check.

2 **Find the answers to these questions.**

1 When did the first movie theater open?
2 How many movie theaters were there by 1907?
3 What did audiences listen to while they were watching silent movies?
4 Why did some actors lose their jobs after 1926?
5 What happened in the 1970s?
6 How will we be able to feel a character's emotions?

3 **BUILD YOUR VOCABULARY Look at verbs 1–4 and find corresponding nouns in the text ending with the suffix *-er* or *-or*.**

1 view 2 produce 3 act 4 project

4 **Write a noun ending with the suffix *-er* or *-or* for each definition. Check your answers in a dictionary.**

1 A person who directs movies is a ___.
2 A person who speaks well is a good ___.
3 A person who conducts an orchestra is a ___.
4 A person who invents things is an ___.
5 A person who paints is a ___.
6 A person who translates is a ___.

5 **YOUR OPINIONS Ask and answer the questions.**

1 Would you enjoy "Smell-O-Vision"? Why do you think that it wasn't successful?
2 Do you prefer going to the movie theater or watching DVDs? Why?
3 What are the advantages and disadvantages of going to the movie theater?
4 Which movies are popular in your country right now? Why?
5 What do you think about movies from your country? Who are the most popular directors?

Moving pictures: technology and the movies

From the early days of silent, black and white movies to our modern digital productions, the movie industry has changed a lot over the last century.

At the beginning of the 20th century, there weren't any movie theaters. When a traveling "picture show" came to a town, people usually watched the short movies in a tent. The first permanent movie theater was Thomas Tally's Electric Theater, which opened in Los Angeles in 1902. By 1907, there were more than 4,000 movie theaters in the U.S., where audiences watched silent comedies, dramas, and news stories, with a pianist providing music.

Color movies delighted viewers when they started to replace black and white movies in the early 1920s, but it was the introduction of sound between 1926 and 1930 which really revolutionized the movies. Genres like musicals and horror movies became popular as movie producers could include songs, dialogues, and sound effects in their "talking pictures." But some actors lost their jobs because they didn't have good voices or simply couldn't act and speak at the same time.

LANGUAGE FOCUS ■ *could, can, will be able to*

I can talk about ability and possibility.

1 Complete the sentences from the text. Then answer the questions.

Past

1 Movie producers ___ include songs.

Present

2 Filmmakers ___ now create very realistic special effects.

Future

3 We'll ___ connect our bodies to special seats.

1 Does *can* express ability or possibility?
2 What are the negative forms of sentences 1–3?
3 Do *can*, *could*, and *will be able to* stay the same with all persons?

More practice ⇨ Workbook page 57

here were various experiments with 3D and with novies with smells ("Smell-O-Vision") in the 1950s and 960s, but they weren't very successful. Movie technology lidn't change much until the 1970s, when surround ound became popular. This made the movie experience nore realistic because sound seemed to come from all lirections. After that, the next real revolution came with computers. Filmmakers can now create very realistic special effects, and computer-generated images have had a big impact, particularly on science fiction movies and animation.

These days, digital projectors produce clearer images, and as 3D technology improves, movies will seem more realistic. It's also possible that with future technology, we'll be able to connect our bodies to special seats and feel the same emotions and sensations as the characters on the screen. But ... will we really want to do that?

2 Complete the sentences with *could*, *couldn't*, *can*, *can't*, *'ll be able to*, and *won't be able to*.

1 Excuse me, I ___ see.
2 I ___ watch movies at home on DVDs.
3 If the movie theater closes next month, we ___ see any new movies.
4 Before 1926, audiences ___ hear actors' voices at the movies.
5 She had a lot of talent. She ___ sing, dance, and act.
6 When I'm a rich and famous star, I ___ choose the characters I want to play.

3 Complete the text with the verbs in the box and the correct forms of *could*, *can*, and *will be able to*.

smell enjoy wear connect feel hear

Movie theaters and the senses

In 1960, a system called "Smell-O-Vision" introduced smells into movie theaters for the movie *Scent of Mystery*. Audiences [1]___ thirty different scents during the movie, but unfortunately the machines were noisy, so some people [2]___ the movie. There were also problems with the first 3D movies because people [3]___ the special glasses for long – they felt sick.

These days, we [4]___ 3D movies without any problems and it's possible that in the movie theaters of the future, we [5]___ the same sensations as the characters. Scientists say that they [6]___ the audience to computers and stimulate emotions in their brains..

4 ACTIVATE Complete the questions with *can*, *could*, or *will be able to*. Then ask and answer with a partner.

1 What type of movies ___ people watch before 1926?
2 What type of movies ___ we ___ watch ten years from now?
3 When ___ we ___ to watch 3D movies on cell phones?
4 ___ you go to the movies every week?
5 ___ you go to the movies alone when you were ten?

Finished?

Write sentences about your past, present, and future abilities.

I couldn't ride a bicycle until I was seven.

VOCABULARY AND LISTENING ■ Books and movies: features

I can understand a program about books and movies.

1 **Check the meaning of the words in the box. Then complete the table.**

~~beginning~~ ending special effects novelist movie director theme subtitles blockbuster bestseller plot scene character biography cast setting script publisher

Books only	Movies only	Both books and movies
		beginning

2 **Match the definitions with words in exercise 1.**

1 All the actors in a movie.
2 A very successful movie.
3 A writer of fiction.
4 A very successful book.
5 The story of a person's life.
6 The written text of a movie.
7 A written translation on the screen.
8 When and where a story takes place.

3 3.04 **Listen to a radio program. Match the topics in the box with the speakers. There are more topics than you need.**

romance wars biography crime plot characters special effects ending setting

1 Emma ___ 2 Josh ___ 3 Amy ___ 4 Luke ___

4 3.04 **Listen again and complete the notes.**

Emma doesn't usually enjoy reading [1]___ books, but she liked *The Catcher in the Rye*. She thought that the [2]___ was realistic.

Josh read *The Time Machine*. This is a classic [3]___ story by the [4]___ H.G. Wells. Josh didn't like the [5]___ or the ending.

Amy read *The Black Magician*, a modern [6]___ trilogy by an [7]___ writer named Trudi Canavan.

Luke likes crime fiction and he enjoyed *The Hound of the Baskervilles* by Arthur Conan Doyle. The main [8]___ is the famous detective Sherlock Holmes.

5 ACTIVATE **Ask and answer the questions.**

1 Which of the books mentioned in *Bookworld* would you (not) like to read? Why?
2 Do the best books and movies have happy endings? Why / Why not?
3 What is more important in a good movie, the special effects or the plot? Why?
4 What do you think about books and movies with historical themes and settings? Why?
5 What do you do if you don't like the beginning of a book or movie?

LANGUAGE FOCUS ■ Second conditional

I can talk about imaginary situations.

1 Complete the second conditional sentences from the listening on page 72 with the words in the box. Then complete the rules with *would*, *wouldn't*, and *simple past*.

'd wouldn't would had did

Situation	Result
If I [1]___ that,	I would make things worse.
If he [2]___ a time machine,	he'd go to the past.
If the school expelled you,	[3]___ you leave home?
Result	**Situation**
I [4]___ go to the past	if I had a time machine.
I [5]___ leave home	if the school expelled me.
Where would you go	if you had a time machine?

RULES

1 We use the second conditional to talk about an imaginary or unlikely situation and to describe its result.
2 We talk about the unlikely or imaginary situation with *if* + ___.
3 We describe the result with ___ or ___ + base form.

More practice ⇨ Workbook page 59

2 Complete the sentences with the second conditional form of the verbs in parentheses.

If you **traveled** (travel) to the past, you'**d learn** (learn) about history.

1 I ___ (enjoy) the book more if I ___ (like) the characters.
2 If it ___ (have) a happy ending, we ___ (not believe) the story.
3 I ___ (not watch) the movie if I ___ (hate) the book.
4 The story ___ (be) more interesting if they ___ (change) the setting.
5 She ___ (not be) happy if you ___ (not go) to the party.
6 If you ___ (buy) him a ticket, he ___ (come) to the movies.

3 Write questions using the second conditional. Then ask and answer.

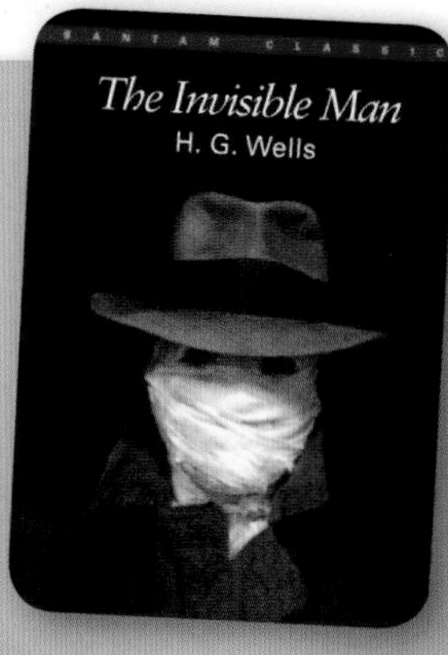

The Invisible Man

1 What (you / do) if (you / become) invisible?

The Time Machine

2 If (you / have) a time machine, where (you / go)?
3 If (you / go) to the past, who (you / meet)?

The Dark Knight

4 If (you / have) a special power, what (it / be)?
5 If (you / be) a superhero, (you / tell) your friends?

Twilight

6 (you / love) a person if (you / discover) he or she was a vampire?

4 ACTIVATE Interview your partner about situations 1–6.

What would you do if you were ...

1 famous?
2 the president?
3 a teacher?
4 your parents?
5 an insect?
6 a writer?

What would you do if you were famous?

If I were famous, I'd live in Hollywood.

Finished?

Write second conditional sentences with the adjectives in the box.

angry happy excited worried scared embarrassed unhappy tired

I'd be angry if I lost my keys.

SPEAKING ■ Expressing preferences and recommending

I can talk about books and movies that I prefer.

1 **Look at the picture. Where are Tom and Caitlin? What are they doing?**

2 3.05 **Listen to the dialogue. What type of movie does Tom choose?**

Tom	Hey, Caitlin, have you seen any good movies recently?
Caitlin	Yes, one or two. Have you?
Tom	No. What about this one? Is it any good?
Caitlin	I'd only recommend that if you like really bad musicals.
Tom	No, I don't want that.
Caitlin	If they had *Avatar*, I'd recommend that, but I can't see it anywhere.
Tom	Yeah, well there's no point in watching it if it isn't in 3D, and I can't do that at home.
Caitlin	No, you're right. It's a great movie to see at the movie theater. Oh, here you are. You might like this. It has great special effects.
Tom	What's that? *Mission to Planet Q*? No, I'm not a big fan of science fiction. I'd prefer a comedy.
Caitlin	A comedy ... um ... OK, well, try this one. It's a really funny story. I think you'll like it.
Tom	OK. I'll trust you. Thanks, Caitlin.
Caitlin	No problem. Enjoy it!

3 3.06 **Study the key phrases. Which phrases respond to recommendations? Who says these phrases in the dialogue? Listen and check. Practice the dialogue with a partner.**

KEY PHRASES ○ Recommending and responding

What about this one?
I'd only recommend that if ... .
I don't want that.
If they had (*Avatar*), I'd recommend that.
You might like ... .
I'm not a big fan of ... .
Try this one.

4 3.07 **Listen to three sentences and choose the correct responses.**

1 a What about comedies? b OK. Thanks. c You might like musicals.
2 a I don't want that. b Oh, here you are. c I'd recommend that.
3 a What's that? b OK. I'll trust you. c No problem.

5 **Think of good and bad movies and books that you know. Complete the table. Then ask and answer with a partner.**

Good movies and books	Bad movies and books

Have you seen / read ... ?

What did you think of it?

I thought it was ...

6 **ACTIVATE** **Prepare a new dialogue with a partner. Talk about movies that you know. Practice your dialogue. Then change roles.**

Pronunciation: Silent letters ⇨ Workbook page 92

WRITING ■ A review of a book or a movie

I can write a book or a movie review.

1 **Read the model text and answer the questions.**

1 Which paragraphs express opinions and which express facts?
2 Which paragraph describes the setting and characters?
3 Which paragraph mentions the theme?
4 Who would enjoy this novel?
5 Why is the plot simple?

2 **Study the key phrases. Which phrases introduce an opinion? Which introduce a fact?**

KEY PHRASES ○ Facts and opinions

I have recently read … .
I'd like to recommend … .
The main characters are … .
The setting is … .
I particularly enjoyed … .
All in all, I (really enjoyed) … .
I'd / I wouldn't change it.

The Boy in the Striped Pajamas

1 I have recently read a book called *The Boy in the Striped Pajamas*. It is a bestseller by an Irish author named John Boyne.

2 I'd like to recommend this book to people who enjoy drama and realism. It's set in Poland during the Second World War and the main characters are two young boys – a German boy named Bruno and a Polish boy named Shmuel. The plot centers on the relationship between the boys and the different situations which they are in.

3 I particularly enjoyed the characters and the theme of friendship in the novel. Some of the scenes are memorable because they're really strong, but the style and plot are very simple because a child narrates the story.

4 All in all, I really enjoyed the novel and I wouldn't change the plot or characters. This is an easy book to read, with a strong ending and a clear message.

Language point: Paragraphs and topic sentences

3 **Find the topic sentences in each paragraph in the model text. Then replace the topic sentences with a–e. There is one sentence that you do not need.**

a The things I liked most about the book were the characters and the theme of friendship.
b The book will appeal to people who like drama and realism.
c In conclusion, I really liked the novel.
d The setting is during the Second World War and the characters are very realistic.
e I'd like to recommend a book which I read recently, called *The Boy in the Striped Pajamas*.

4 ACTIVATE **Follow the steps in the writing guide.**

○ WRITING GUIDE

A TASK

Write a review of a book or a movie which you enjoyed.

B THINK AND PLAN

1 What's the name of the book or movie?
2 Who wrote it / starred in it / directed it?
3 What's the setting and who are the main characters?
4 What did you like most about it?
5 Does it have a good plot or any very memorable scenes?
6 What did you think of it overall?
7 Would you change any part of it?

C WRITE

Paragraph 1: Introduction
I'd like to recommend …
Paragraph 2: Details
The book / movie is …
Paragraph 3: Opinions
The things I liked most …
Paragraph 4: Conclusion
All in all, …

D CHECK

- order and content of paragraphs
- phrases for facts and opinions
- book and movie vocabulary

REVIEW Unit 7

Vocabulary

1 Match the sentences with the words in the box.

fantasy	comedy	science fiction	horror
musical	adventure		

1 I nearly fell off my seat. It was so funny! ___
2 I'm not into magicians and strange talking animals. ___
3 It was really scary. I couldn't sleep. ___
4 I love exciting stories and that one was fantastic. ___
5 The setting was on a strange planet in the year 3010. ___
6 The music was good, but the story was terrible! ___

2 Complete the text with the words in the box.

reader	character	ending	beginning
novelist	themes	setting	bestseller

the CATCHER in the RYE
a novel by J. D. SALINGER

The American [1]___ J.D. Salinger wrote *The Catcher in the Rye* in 1951. It became a [2]___ all over the world. The main [3]___ is a teenager named Holden Caulfield. The [4]___ is the U.S. in the 1950s. At the [5]___ of the story, Holden is at boarding school. The school expels him and the story is about three days he spends alone in New York. The [6]___ of the book are growing up and how false adults can be. The [7]___ is a little mysterious because the [8]___ isn't sure what will happen to Holden.

Language focus

3 Complete the sentences with *could, couldn't, can, can't, will be able to,* and *won't be able to.*

1 It's a terrible movie because the hero ___ act!
2 When I was younger, I ___ dance at all.
3 Now I ___ dance and sing very well.
4 I'm afraid we ___ see the movie next week. We're taking a trip.
5 I ___ run very fast when I was young, but I'm too old now.
6 Movie directors ___ do amazing things in the future.

4 Complete the second conditional sentences with the correct form of the verbs in parentheses.

I *'d watch* (watch) *Avatar* if I *had* (have) the DVD.

1 I ___ (not go) to see a movie if it ___ (have) bad reviews.
2 If I ___ (be) a movie director, I ___ (make) war movies.
3 If the director ___ (have) more money, he ___ (choose) better actors.
4 You ___ (not like) the story if it ___ (have) a happy ending.
5 If I ___ (meet) Brad Pitt, I ___ (not know) what to say to him.

5 Write questions for the sentences in exercise 4.

If you had the DVD, would you watch Avatar?

Communication

6 Match questions 1–7 with the responses a–g.

1 Do you prefer comedies or westerns?
2 Do you enjoy reading thrillers?
3 What would you prefer to see?
4 Is this book any good?
5 Would you recommend this movie?
6 Have you read any good books recently?
7 What about this movie?

a I don't like it.
b No, I don't.
c No, I wouldn't. It isn't very good.
d I'd prefer to see a comedy.
e I don't know. I haven't read it.
f I like them both.
g Yes, I have, *Twilight*.

Listening

7 3.08 Listen and choose the correct words.

1 Sally has a **detective** / **spy** novel to read for school.
2 She **hates** / **loves** reading.
3 Dan **has** / **hasn't** seen the movie *Sherlock Holmes*.
4 Conan Doyle **didn't write** / **wrote** the plot of the movie.
5 Dan preferred the **movie** / **book**.
6 Sally **would** / **wouldn't** read it if it wasn't for school.

PROJECT A movie poster

1 Look at the movie poster. Find out who directed the movie and where the special effects were made.

AVATAR

he science fiction blockbuster of all time

Directed by: James Cameron
Special visual effects by: Welta Digital, New Zealand
Music by: James Horner
Starring: Sam Worthington and Zoe Saldana

lot summary

vatar is an epic 3D science fiction movie which takes place in ne future on a planet called Pandora. It is a world of beautiful orests and strange creatures and aliens called Na'vi. Greedy umans want valuable material on the planet and they attack the eaceful Na'vi. *Avatar* is the story of an American soldier who falls n love with an alien and leads the battle against his own people.

pecial effects

ameron wrote the story of *Avatar* in 1994, but he couldn't make ne movie then because the technology he needed didn't exist. He ad to wait another twelve years for the new 3D technology. The ew Zealand company which made The Lord of the Rings did the pecial effects for *Avatar*.

Sam Worthington

Sam Worthington is an Australian actor who was born in the U.K. He plays the role of the American soldier who refuses to attack the Na'vi people. Sam was a construction worker before he became an actor and he is into surfing. He auditioned for James Bond, but didn't get the part.

Zoe Saldana

Zoe Saldana is an American actress who plays the role of the Na'vi princess. Zoe had to learn martial arts, archery, and horseback riding for the role. She loves science fiction and she has also acted in a recent *Star Trek* movie. She can speak Spanish because her father comes from the Dominican Republic.

2 Make a poster for a movie. Follow the steps in the project checklist.

PROJECT CHECKLIST

1. Choose a movie you have seen or would like to see.
2. Find information about it on the Internet.
3. Make a poster for the movie. Include information about: the director, the special effects, the music, the plot, and the main characters.
4. Write a short plot summary and descriptions of the stars.
5. Write about the special effects or another important feature of the movie.
6. Find some pictures of the movie on the Internet or in magazines.

3 Display your posters in the classroom. Did any other students choose the same movie as you?

Art

Start thinking

1 Do you know any artists or paintings?
2 What artists are / were from your country?
3 What are the most important art museums in your city or country?

Aims

Communication: I can ...

- talk about artists and works of art.
- understand a text about Dada art.
- use the past passive to talk about art.
- describe art.
- ask and answer quiz questions using the passive.
- express opinions and doubts.
- write about a piece of art.

Vocabulary

- Nouns: art
- Adjectives: describing art

Language focus

- Present passive: affirmative and negative
- Past passive: affirmative and negative
- Present and past passive: affirmative, negative, and questions

Reach Out Options

Extra listening and speaking
Discussing a picture
Page 95

Curriculum extra
Visual arts: Art movements of the 20th century
Page 103

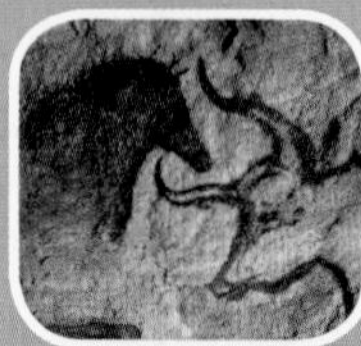

Culture
Graffiti artists – past and present
Page 111

Vocabulary bank
Synonyms; Works of art
Page 119

VOCABULARY AND LANGUAGE FOCUS

Nouns: art

I can talk about artists and works of art.

1 Complete the table with the words in the box. Which word doesn't go in any list? Then do the *Art Quiz* with a partner.

~~painting~~ sculpture gallery landscape auction critic art movement masterpiece museum exhibition collector portrait

Places	People	Works of art	Events
		painting	

Pronunciation: Word stress ⇨ Workbook page 92

2 3.14 Listen and check your answers to the quiz. How many did you answer correctly?

3 Write definitions of six of the words from exercise 1. Then work in pairs. Guess the words from your partner's definitions.

It's a person who collects things.
A collector.

Art Quiz

1 Many Impressionist paintings are exhibited in a museum in Paris.
The Impressionists were ...
a part of an art movement.
b a group of critics.
c galleries for special paintings.

The Mulberry Tree

The Drachenfels

2 This painting by J.M.W. Turner shows his skill as a ...
a critic.
b landscape artist.
c portrait artist.

3 A collector bought this painting at an auction for ...
a over $4,000,000.
b over $14,000,000.
c over $43,000,000.

The Nympheas

Present passive: affirmative and negative

4 **Complete the sentences. Use the quiz to help you.**

Passive affirmative
It ***is painted*** on walls and buildings.
Many Impressionist paintings [1]___ in a museum in Paris.

Passive negative
Sculptures [2]___ from gold.
His graffiti [3]___ in museums.

Active affirmative
This painting [4]___ Turner's skill as a landscape artist.

Active negative
People [5]___ Banksy's graffiti art.

Horse

4 This is an exhibition of a sculpture by Fernando Botero. Sculptures aren't usually made from ...

a gold.
b marble.
c bronze.

5 Leonardo da Vinci painted this masterpiece. It is called ...

a *Mona's Smile.*
b *Mona Lisa.*
c *Mona Lisa's Smile.*

Mona Lisa

Maid Sweeping

6 Banksy is a British street artist. His graffiti isn't found in museums because ...

a it isn't art.
b it is painted on walls and buildings.
c people don't like it.

5 **Study the passive sentences in exercise 4 and complete the rules with the words in the box.**

past participle   is   am not   aren't

RULES

1 We form the present passive affirmative with *am* / ___ / *are* + past participle.
2 We form the present passive negative with ___ / *isn't* / ___ + ___.

More practice ⇨ Workbook page 65

6 **Make sentences using the present passive.**

1 Portraits ___ very often these days. (not paint)
2 Modern art ___ by a lot of people. (criticize)
3 This sculpture ___ from bronze. (make)
4 His greatest masterpiece ___ in the exhibition. (not show)
5 Some artists ___ by society. (not accept)
6 Many famous paintings ___ by museums. (not own)

7 **Complete the quiz sentences with passive forms of the verbs in the box. Then write your answers to the quiz.**

sell   buy   speak   make   use   set   mix

1 This language ___ in Peru.
2 Omelets ___ with these.
3 *The Boy in the Striped Pajamas* ___ in this country.
4 When these colors ___, they make purple.
5 Paintings ___ and ___ in these places.
6 These glass objects ___ when we drink.

8 ACTIVATE **Work in pairs. Make more quiz sentences using the verbs in exercise 7. Then exchange your sentences with another pair.**

These things are sold in a music store.

Finished?

Write sentences about the works of art on this page. Write why you like or dislike them.

READING ■ Dada

I can understand a text about Dada art.

1 **Check the meaning of the words in blue in the text. What do you think of the pieces of art on this page?**

2 3.15 **Read and listen to the text. Choose the correct answers.**

1 Critics in the past were ___ Dada.
 a indifferent to
 b positive about
 c negative about

2 The author wrote the text to ___.
 a criticize
 b inform
 c amuse

3 **Read the text again. Write *true* or *false*. Correct the false sentences.**

1 The Dada movement was started by Marcel Duchamp.
2 There were writers in the Dada movement.
3 Dada rejected ideas which artists had in the past.
4 Dada artists wanted people to think about art.
5 *Fountain* was rejected because Duchamp used a false name.
6 Critics' opinions about Dada have become more negative.

4 **BUILD YOUR VOCABULARY Find synonyms in the text for 1–6.**

1 aims (paragraph 1)
2 straightforward (paragraph 1)
3 features (paragraph 2)
4 common (paragraph 2)
5 most unhealthy (paragraph 3)
6 important (paragraph 3)

5 **Write synonyms for the words in the box.**

~~original~~ attractive actually intelligent unusual adore excellent

original = very different

6 **YOUR OPINIONS Ask and answer the questions.**

1 Answer the questions in the introduction of the text.
2 Why do you think Duchamp's work shocked people? What's your opinion?
3 How do writers, artists, or musicians shock people these days?
4 What would you paint if you were an artist?
5 What are your favorite types of art: sculptures, portraits, abstract, other?

DadA

Art, because the artist says it's art

Can a toilet be a work of art? What about putting a bicycle wheel on a stool? Is that art? Anyone can do it. What is art? Dada art makes people think.

Bicycle Wheel

Dada was an art movement which was started by a group of artists during the First World War. The origin of the name Dada isn't certain, but the objectives of the movement were clear: through art and literature, they protested against the war and against conservative ideas. They rejected traditions and traditional art because, for them, everything was boring. They wanted to start something new.

Dada was sometimes fun, often provocative, and always original, and you can see all of these characteristics in the work of the French artist Marcel Duchamp. In his opinion, art was usually created for the eyes, but he wanted to create art for the mind. When he added a mustache to a copy of the *Mona Lisa* in 1919, it was an anti-art joke, and with his *Bicycle Wheel* (1913), he was saying, "this is art because the artist says it's art." For Duchamp, everyday objects could be art. In 1917, he inverted a urinal, signed it with a false name, called it *Fountain*, and sent it to an exhibition. It was rejected.

LANGUAGE FOCUS ■ Past passive: affirmative and negative

I can use the past passive to talk about art.

1 Study the sentences in the tables. How do we form the negative of past passive sentences? Complete the rules.

Active	Subject	Active verb	Object
	A group of artists	started	Dada.
	Most critics	rejected	Dada works of art.
	Picasso	didn't start	Dada.

Passive	Subject	*be* + past participle	*by* + agent
	Dada	was started	by a group of artists.
	Dada works of art	were rejected	by most critics.
	Dada	wasn't started	by Picasso.

RULES

When we change a sentence from active to passive:

1 The object of the active sentence becomes the ___ in the passive.
2 The subject in the active sentence becomes the ___ in the passive.
3 The tense of the verb *be* in the passive is the same as the tense of the ___ verb.
4 If we include the agent in the passive, we need the word ___.

More practice ⇨ Workbook page 65

Mona Lisa with mustache

In fact, Dada works of art were rejected by most critics. Their everyday objects, which they called "readymades," were completely different from the traditional world of paintings and sculptures. One critic said that Dada was the "sickest and most destructive thing" invented by man. But opinions change and eighty-seven years later, a group of five hundred British critics voted *Fountain* "the most influential work of modern art." In fact, if you look at some of the stranger pieces of art today, you can see the influence of Dada. Thanks to Dada, everything can be art now. There are no rules.

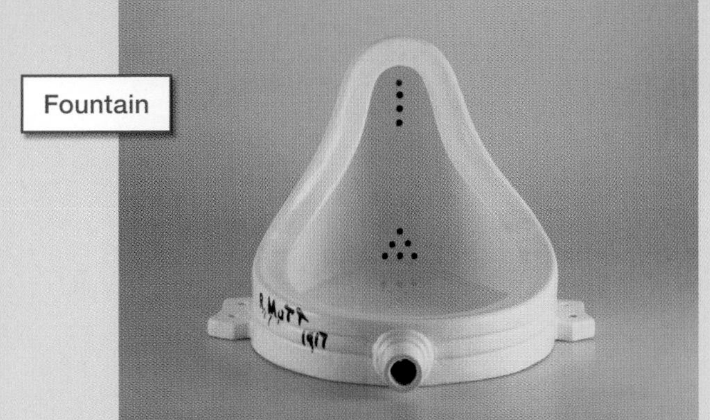

Fountain

2 **Complete the passive sentences with the verbs in parentheses.**

1 The Surrealists ___ by Dada artists. (influence)
2 Some unusual objects ___ by Surrealist artists. (create)
3 The Surrealist movement ___ by André Breton. (start)
4 *Le Déjeuner en fourrure* ___ by Meret Oppenheim. (make)
5 The *Mona Lisa* ___ by Picasso. (not paint)
6 *Fountain* ___ in an exhibition because the organizers didn't like it. (not show).

Le Déjeuner en fourrure

3 ACTIVATE **Choose a piece of art on pages 78–81 and make passive sentences using the verbs in the box. Take turns to guess the piece of art with a partner.**

paint   sell   make   find   exhibit   buy

It was painted a long time ago.

Is it The Mulberry Tree?

Finished?

Write passive sentences about other famous things. Think of books, movies, buildings, sculptures, and inventions.

Hamlet was written by Shakespeare.

STUDY STRATEGY ☐ Marking word stress

1 3.16 **Check the meaning of the words in the box. Then listen and underline the stressed syllable in each word. Remember to do this when you learn new vocabulary.**

beautiful

~~beautiful~~ controversial amusing shocking imaginative ridiculous traditional dull colorful original strange provocative

2 **Choose six adjectives. Write sentences about things they can describe.**

The Harry Potter books are very imaginative.

3 3.17 **Look at pictures A–D. Then listen to the *Arts Spectrum* podcast. In what order are the artists mentioned? Is the prize always given to a painter?**

4 3.17 **Listen again and choose the correct answers.**

1 The Turner Prize is named after a …
  a young artist. b British painter. c modern sculptor.
2 What kind of art often wins?
  a abstract b modern c conceptual
3 What was the boat made from in *Shedboatshed*?
  a a shed b another boat c recycled trash
4 Why is the Turner Prize criticized?
  a It isn't shocking. b It isn't art. c It isn't always won by conceptual artists.
5 What is Beth's opinion of the Turner Prize?
  a Some of the art that is nominated is shocking.
  b Original and imaginative art is presented.
  c It's interesting, but some pieces are ridiculous.

5 ACTIVATE **Look at the pieces of art in this unit. Choose one or more adjectives from exercise 1 to describe each picture. Then compare your ideas with a partner.**

The Drachenfels is traditional and beautiful.

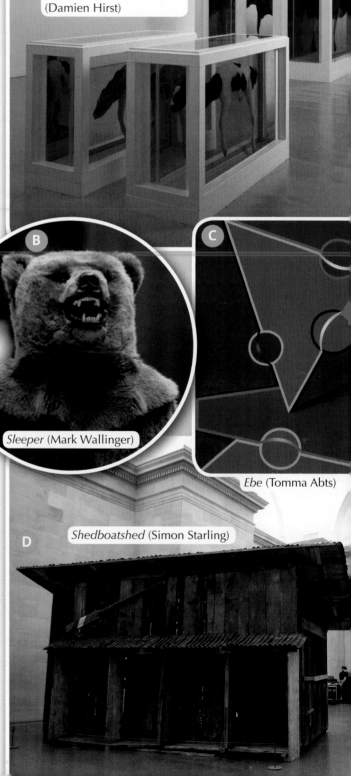

ARTS SPECTRUM Podcast

The Turner Prize – original or ridiculous?

Leo Walker and Beth Jones discuss the most famous and controversial art prize in Britain.

A *Mother and Child Divided* (Damien Hirst)

B *Sleeper* (Mark Wallinger)

C *Ebe* (Tomma Abts)

D *Shedboatshed* (Simon Starling)

LANGUAGE FOCUS ■ Present and past passive: affirmative, negative, and questions

I can ask and answer quiz questions using the passive.

8

1 Complete the passive sentences a–f from the listening on page 82 with the words in the box. Then answer questions 1–4.

was (x2) nominated is (x2) were

a It ___ preserved in liquid.
b It ___ won by Tomma Abts for her abstract paintings.
c ___ the Turner Prize always given to a painter?
d What kind of art is ___ for the prize?
e Why ___ people shocked by Damien Hirst's cow?
f ___ the *Shedboatshed* made of recycled wood?

1 Which sentences are in the past?
2 Which sentences are in the present?
3 Which word is the same in all forms?
4 How are questions formed?

More practice ⇨ Workbook page 67

2 Complete the dialogue with the verbs in parentheses. Use the present and past passive.

John When was the *Mona Lisa* painted?
Laura It [1]___ by Leonardo da Vinci in the 16th century. (paint)
John Where was it kept?
Laura It [2]___ by the King of France and it [3]___ in the Louvre Museum in Paris. (buy, put)
John What happened in 1911?
Laura The painting [4]___ from the museum. (steal)
John When was it found?
Laura It [5]___ two years later and a museum worker confessed to the crime. (find)
John Is the painting back in the Louvre Museum now?
Laura Yes, and it [6]___ by six million people each year, but the paintings in the Louvre [7]___ very well now. (see, protect)

3 Write questions in the passive about the information in blue in the text below. Then ask and answer with a partner.

When ... ?
When was the Tate Modern opened?

1 What ___?
2 Where ___?
3 How much ___?
4 Who ___?
5 When ___?
6 What ___?

4 Write six quiz questions using the words in the box.

make play speak write paint

What is pizza made from?

5 ACTIVATE Study the key phrases. Which phrase is for answering a question? Work in pairs and ask and answer your quiz questions in exercise 4.

KEY PHRASES ▢ Doing a quiz

What's your next question?
OK. You start.
I think the answer's ... .
That's right. Well done.
No, sorry. Good try.
OK. It's your turn.

▢ *Finished?*
Look through this book and write a quiz. Use the present and past passive.
How are marine animals affected by plastic?

Guggenheim, Bilbao

Great Museums

The Tate Modern in London was opened as an art museum in 2000. In the past, the building was used [1]as a power station. Bigger works of art are now exhibited [2]in a massive hall. Visitors [3]aren't charged any money to go into the gallery.

The Guggenheim Museum in Bilbao was designed by [4]architect Frank Gehry and it was built [5]between 1994 and 1997. It's used for [6]exhibitions and conferences. It's also great to look at and it's a nice place to meet.

Tate Modern, London

SPEAKING ■ Expressing doubt

I can express opinions and doubts.

1 Look at the picture. What kind of art is the painting? Do you like it?

2 3.18 Listen to the dialogue. Why does Lucy dislike the picture?

Mom Look, Lucy. I got this picture this morning.
Lucy It reminds me of a Picasso painting.
Mom That's because it *is* a Picasso! What do you think?
Lucy It doesn't look like a real face. What on earth is that?
Mom It's a woman. It's abstract art. Don't you like it?
Lucy Mmm. I'm not convinced.
Mom Don't you think it's interesting?
Lucy Um, sort of, but I'm not sure about the face – it looks a little crazy. In fact, it looks as if a child painted it!
Mom Oh, come on! It isn't that bad. It's really colorful. It's good to have a new picture, anyway.
Lucy I suppose so.
Mom I'm sure it'll grow on you.
Lucy OK. We'll see.

3 3.19 Study the key phrases. Who says the phrases? Listen and check. Practice the dialogue with a partner.

KEY PHRASES ▢ Describing art

It reminds me of ... .
It doesn't look like a ... .
What on earth is that?
I'm not sure about ... .
It looks (a little crazy).
It looks as if (a child painted it).

4 3.20 Look at the words in blue in the dialogue in exercise 2. What do they mean? Then complete the mini-dialogue with *look* and *looks like*. Listen and check.

Jack [1]___, Flora. What do you think of this painting?
Flora I'm not sure. It [2]___ a little strange. It [3]___ a girl with a baby.
Jack No, it [4]___ a doll.
Flora It reminds me of a Picasso painting.
Jack That's because it *is* a Picasso!

5 Look at the picture of *Compression*. Change the words in blue in the dialogue in exercise 4 and practice a new mini-dialogue with a partner.

6 ACTIVATE Look at *The Scream* and prepare a new dialogue with a partner. Use the key phrases and ideas from exercise 4 or your own ideas. Practice your dialogue. Then change roles and practice another dialogue about *Compression*.

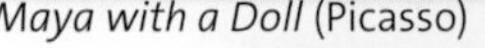

Maya with a Doll (Picasso)

The Scream (Munch)

Compression (César)

WRITING ■ A description of a piece of art

I can write about a piece of art.

8

1 Read the model text and match the paragraphs 1–3 with the topics a–d. There is one topic that you do not need.

a an art movement
b historical details
c the painter
d a description

2 Answer the questions.

1 When was this picture painted?
2 What dramatic feature is in the foreground?
3 What adjectives describe Surrealist art?
4 When was the painting first exhibited?
5 Where can you see the painting today?

The Persistence of Memory

1 *The Persistence of Memory* was painted by Salvador Dalí in 1931. It is an oil painting and it shows a landscape. The unusual scenery includes melting watches in the foreground, and in the background there are cliffs. It is said that he saw a round camembert cheese melting in the hot sun. It inspired him to paint this picture.

2 This type of work is typical of Surrealism, an art movement which started in France in the 1920s. The Surrealists used intense colors and bizarre images. Their work sometimes shows dream scenes or imaginative landscapes.

3 *The Persistence of Memory* was first exhibited in 1931, where it was bought by an American collector for $250. It was later sold and donated to the Museum of Modern Art in New York, where it is now kept.

3 Study the key phrases. Which phrases describe the painting?

KEY PHRASES ○ Describing a painting

The scenery / composition includes … .
… in the foreground / background … .
(*The Persistence of Memory*) was first exhibited … .
It is said that … .
This type of work is typical of … .
Their work sometimes shows … .

Language point: Using synonyms

4 Look at the model text again and find synonyms for the adjectives in blue in a–d. Then choose synonyms for the words in blue in the text below.

a weird scenery
b bright colors
c strange images
d creative landscapes

The artist showed the world in a [1]new (original / controversial) way and some of his pictures are very [2]funny (amusing / provocative). But in this picture, the colors are really [3]dark (elegant / sombre) and the ants [4]represent (describe / symbolize) death.

5 **ACTIVATE** Follow the steps in the writing guide.

○ WRITING GUIDE

A TASK

Find information about a famous piece of art, or look at the painting in the picture with Mom and Lucy on page 84 and the notes about it below. Write a text about the piece of art.

Notes on *Dora Maar au Chat* (Picasso):
Painted 1941.
Cubism, France 1907. Artists looked at subjects from different perspectives and used geometric shapes.
Sold to collectors; not exhibited until 2005; sold in 2006 for over $95 million; now owned by private collector.

B THINK AND PLAN

1 Who was the work created by and when?
2 What does the work of art show?
3 What art movement is this typical of?
4 What is typical of this art movement?
5 When was the work first exhibited?
6 When was it last sold and where is it kept?

C WRITE

Paragraph 1: The work of art
… was painted / made by …
Paragraph 2: The art movement
This type of work is typical of …
Paragraph 3: History of the work
… was first exhibited in …

D CHECK

- synonyms
- the passive

REVIEW Unit 8

Vocabulary

1 Choose the correct words.

1 She sold the painting at **an auction** / **a portrait**.
2 Most of the **masterpieces** / **critics** liked his new exhibition.
3 He painted a good **landscape** / **portrait** of his father.
4 Surrealism was **a masterpiece** / **an art movement**.
5 She is showing her paintings in **a gallery** / **an auction**.
6 A lot of his **sculptures** / **paintings** are made from bronze.

2 Match the adjectives with the sentences.

strange traditional shocking dull ridiculous amusing colorful original provocative

1 I've never seen anything like it before.
2 It isn't very exciting.
3 What do you think it is? I have no idea.
4 Wow! Look at those bright blues and reds.
5 It looks like any other landscape painting.
6 How terrible! That isn't art!
7 The painter definitely has a good sense of humor.
8 I don't understand why that is in the exhibition. It's just stupid.
9 He was an artist who made people think.

Language focus

3 Complete the sentences with the present or past forms of the passive.

1 The masterpiece ___ by the artist in the 19th century. (paint)
2 Today, some artists ___ by society. (not accept)
3 The museum ___ by the president last weekend. (open)
4 The painting ___ by a gallery. (not buy)
5 During the war, paintings ___ by some collectors. (hide)
6 The artist ___ by the critics for many years. (not mention)
7 Today, most of his sculptures ___ by a New York museum. (own)
8 Conceptual art ___ by many people. (appreciate)

4 Make the active sentences passive.

Picasso painted *Guernica*.
***Guernica* was painted by Picasso.**

1 Dada artists influenced the Surrealists.
2 Surrealist artists created some unusual objects.
3 André Breton started the Surrealist movement.
4 Many people don't understand conceptual art.
5 Lots of people visit the museum every year.
6 They didn't show the portrait in the exhibition.

5 Write questions and answers for the sentences in exercise 4. Use the past passive.

Was *Guernica* painted by Picasso? Yes, it was.

Communication

6 Complete the dialogue with the phrases in the box.

like I'm not sure that bad looks as if Look at grow looks reminds me

Brian This is interesting. What do you think?
Julia It's original, but [1]___ I like it.
Brian It looks [2]___ an animal.
Julia It [3]___ of a Dalí painting.
Brian Yes, it [4]___ a little strange.
Julia [5]___ this one over here. It's very unusual.
Brian I don't like that at all. It [6]___ a child painted it.
Julia Oh, come on! It isn't [7]___. Don't you think it's colorful?
Brian Yes, but the colors are all over the place!
Julia Well, I love it. And I'm sure it'll [8]___ on you!

Listening

7 3.21 **Listen to a conversation and complete the text.**

The Scream was painted by Edvard Munch in [1]___. There are [2]___ versions of *The Scream* and three of them are in [3]___ museums. One of the paintings was [4]___ from the Munch Museum in Oslo in [5]___, but the thieves couldn't sell it. Police found the painting in [6]___. Munch belonged to the Expressionist art [7]___. Expressionist [8]___ are interested in feelings, and their paintings don't look like real life.

Listening

1 Look at the pictures and answer the questions.

1 What do the pictures show?
2 Which would you most / least like to see?
3 Which is the strangest? Why?
4 How would you describe these art forms: art or entertainment?
5 Which is the most / least popular with young people? Why?

2 3.22 **Listen to a conversation. Where are Jessica and Jaden?**

3 3.22 **Listen again and complete the sentences.**

1 ___ prefers modern art.
2 The Museum of Modern Art has a lot of ___ art.
3 The painting of the horse looks like a ___.
4 Jessica says that the *Whistlejacket* was Stubbs's ___.
5 ___ wants to buy a poster at the museum store.
6 They decide to visit a temporary ___.
7 Lauren thinks the Frick Collection is ___.
8 Lauren has a ___ of the *Whistlejacket* in her room.

Speaking

4 Work in pairs and prepare a conversation. Imagine you went to a cultural / artistic event or a place in New York City / a city in your country. Answer the questions.

1 Where did you go? Why?
2 What did you see there?
3 What was it like?
4 Who was it created by?
5 Would you recommend it to a friend? Why / Why not?

5 Have a conversation. Use your ideas in exercise 4 and the chart below to help you. One of you is A and one of you is B. Change roles.

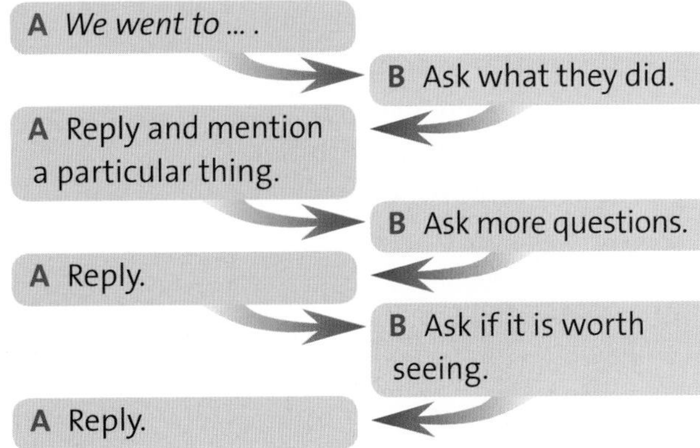

A *We went to ... .*
B Ask what they did.
A Reply and mention a particular thing.
B Ask more questions.
A Reply.
B Ask if it is worth seeing.
A Reply.

Writing

6 Write a description of a cultural or artistic event. Include background information about the event. Use the questions in exercise 4 to help you. Say whether you would recommend this event to someone. Begin like this:

Last week, I visited ... . I saw ... there. It was created by ... .

EXTRA LISTENING AND SPEAKING ■ Deciding what to watch on TV

I can talk about and choose TV programs.

1 Look at the TV guide. Do you know any of the programs? What types of program are they?

	Channel 2	Channel 5	Channel 7	Channel 12	Channel 17
7:30	The Weakest Link	Natural World	The Chart Show	The Simpsons	The Vampire Diaries
8:00	The Office	News at 8		Friends	World Cup Soccer: Japan versus Australia
8:30		Olympic Special	Who Wants to Be a Millionaire?		
9:00	90210			Big Brother	

2 1.16 **Listen to a conversation between Nicola and Martin. Which programs from the TV guide do they mention?**

3 1.16 **Study the key phrases. Then listen to the conversation again and answer the questions.**

KEY PHRASES ○ Discussing what to watch

What time is it on?
What's on tonight?
What else is on?
I (don't) feel like watching ... .
Is there a ... on?

1 Where do they find the TV guide?
   a Under the remote control.
   b Under the sofa.
   c Under a magazine.
2 When's the transportation documentary on?
   a Tuesday.
   b Wednesday.
   c Thursday.
3 What type of program is *90210*?
   a A drama series.
   b A quiz show.
   c A reality show.
4 Martin wants to watch
   a a reality show.
   b a funny program.
   c a quiz show.
5 What time is it now?
   a Just before 7:30.
   b About 8:00.
   c Just after 7:30.

4 1.17 **Listen. Then practice the dialogue with a partner.**

Martin What's on tonight?
Nicola *The Weakest Link* is on at 7:30 on Channel 2.
Martin No, I don't feel like watching a quiz show. What else is on?
Nicola There's *The Chart Show*. That's on at 7:30 on Channel 7.
Martin I'm not sure. I feel like watching some sports. Is there a sports program on?
Nicola Yes, *Olympic Special* is on at 8:30 on Channel 5.
Martin Great! Let's watch that!

5 ACTIVATE **Change the words in blue in exercise 4 using the programs in the TV guide. Then practice your new dialogue with a partner.**

Reach Out Options

EXTRA LISTENING AND SPEAKING ■ Explaining what you want to buy

2

I can ask about and buy things in a store.

1 **Use the words in the table to make objects that you can buy. Then match them with objects A–H.**

a	tube box bottle can package bar	of	deodorant shampoo batteries toothpaste soap aspirin dishwashing detergent light bulbs

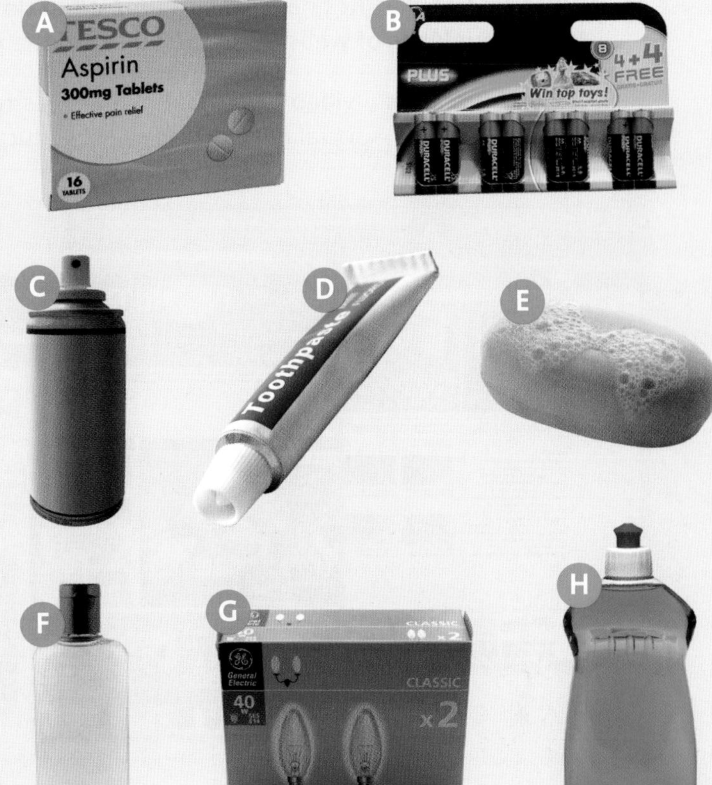

2 1.33 **Listen to two conversations. Which objects from exercise 1 do the customers buy?**

3 1.33 **Study the key phrases. Then listen to the conversations again. Complete the table below with the missing information.**

KEY PHRASES ○ Asking about things in a store

Can I help you?
I need something for … .
Is this what you mean?
You use it for … .
Which type do you want?

Object:	aspirin
Quantity:	1___
Box size:	2___
Price:	$3.08

Object:	toothpaste
Type:	3___
Tube size:	4___
Price:	5___

4 1.34 **Listen. Then practice the dialogue.**

Assistant Can I help you?
Customer Yes, I need something for making light. I'm sorry, I can't remember the word!
Assistant Light bulbs? Is that what you mean?
Customer Yes, light bulbs!
Assistant Which type do you want? 60 watt or 100 watt?
Customer 60 watt, please.
Assistant How many do you need?
Customer One box, please.
Assistant OK. One box of light bulbs. That's $1.18, please.

5 ACTIVATE **Change the words in blue in exercise 4 using the objects in exercise 1 or your own ideas. Then practice your new dialogue with a partner.**

EXTRA LISTENING AND SPEAKING ■ Talking about websites

I can talk about websites, and say e-mail and website addresses.

1 **What kind of websites have you visited? What do you think of them? Match four kinds of websites in the box with the pictures A–D.**

music websites video sites online games sites chat rooms
news websites social networking sites educational websites

2 1.44 **Study the key phrases. Then listen and write the website and e-mail addresses.**

KEY PHRASES ▢ Saying website and e-mail addresses

www = double u, double u, double u
. = dot
_ = underscore
@ = at
- = dash
/ = forward slash
That's all one word.

3 2.02 **Listen to a conversation. Which e-mail address and website does Jade mention?**

4 2.02 **Listen again and write *true* or *false* for 1–5. Correct the false sentences.**

1 Derek has posted a funny video on a website.
2 He offers to e-mail the website address to Jade.
3 Jade has changed her e-mail address.
4 Derek has done his essay.
5 Jade used a book to help her with her homework.

5 **Answer the questions.**

1 What are your favorite websites? Why?
2 What websites do you use to find information for school work?
3 What are the most useful websites that you know?
4 Do you listen to music or watch videos on websites? If so, which websites do you like?
5 Do you or your friends have your own websites? What are they?
6 What websites have you recommended to friends?

6 2.03 **Listen. Then practice the dialogue with a partner.**

Jade Have you seen that awesome British music website?
Derek Which website is that?
Jade It's www.ukcoolmusic.com.
Derek No, I haven't. Is it good?
Jade Yes, it's great. There are album reviews, concert dates, and interviews with bands. There's a message board, too.
Derek It sounds great. Can you e-mail me the link?
Jade Sure. What's your e-mail address?
Derek It's derek_beck@ymail.com.

7 ACTIVATE **Think of a website you know. Change the words in blue in exercise 6. Then practice your new dialogue with a partner.**

EXTRA LISTENING AND SPEAKING ■ Describing people

4

I can describe people.

1 **Look at the picture and describe the people. Use the words in the box.**

He has dark hair.

serious friendly long tall dark shy pretty good-looking blond confident

4 2.16 **Complete the table. Order the adjectives in 1–4. Then listen and check.**

1 curly / long
2 straight / dark
3 red / very short
4 wavy / long / blond

length	style	color	
			hair

2 2.15 **Listen to a conversation between Matt and Sean. Which of the people in the picture are they talking about?**

3 2.15 **Study the key phrases. Then listen to the conversation again and answer the questions.**

KEY PHRASES ▢ Describing people

I recognize the name.
I can't picture him.
What does she look like?
I know who you mean.
Isn't he ... ?

1 What's Sean doing when Matt arrives?
2 What does Matt ask about Suzie's clothes?
3 What does Matt think about Suzie's personality?
4 What does Sean say about Suzie's personality?

5 2.17 **Listen. Then practice the dialogue.**

Carrie Do you know Jacob Lewis?
Emily I recognize the name, but I can't picture him. What does he look like?
Carrie He isn't very tall and he has short, red hair.
Emily Is he friendly?
Carrie Yes, he's really friendly.
Emily I think I know who you mean. Does he usually wear a blue scarf?
Carrie Yes, that's him.
Emily Isn't he from Atlanta?
Carrie Yes, that's right.

6 ACTIVATE **Change the words in blue in exercise 5 using information about someone you know. Then practice your new dialogue with a partner.**

EXTRA LISTENING AND SPEAKING ■ Talking about your school

I can talk about my school.

1 Match pictures A–D with four of the topics from the box.

wearing a school uniform   bullying   cheating   doing homework
studying for tests   school lunches   sports   class size

C

2 2.29 Listen to an interview with James and Clare. Which topics from the box in exercise 1 do they mention?

3 2.29 Study the key phrases. Then listen to the interview again and choose the correct answers.

KEY PHRASES ▢ Talking about problems at school

Is there a problem with ... ?
There's been a problem in my school with ... .
How do you feel about ... ?
How do you think your school can improve?
We should definitely ... .

1 What does Clare say about her school?
  a It's coed. b It's a high school.
  c It's single-sex.
2 Which school has a problem with bullying?
  a Clare's school b James' school
  c both schools
3 What does James say about homework?
  a There's the right amount.
  b There's too much. c There isn't enough.
4 What does Clare want to stop?
  a hockey b winter sports
  c sports outside in winter
5 James says that there's a problem with ___ in his school.
  a bad teachers b difficult students
  c big classes

4 2.30 Listen. Then practice the dialogue.

Polly Is there a problem with cheating in your school?
Olivia Sometimes. Some students write things on their hands when they have a test!
Polly Do you have to wear a school uniform?
Olivia No, we don't.
Polly Do you think that your school should have a uniform?
Olivia Yes, because I think it's nice when everyone looks the same.
Polly How do you think your school can improve?
Olivia In my school, we have to buy lunch at the school cafeteria and it isn't very good. I think we should have better food, because you work better if you have a good lunch!

5 ACTIVATE **Prepare answers to the questions in** blue **in exercise 4 using ideas about your school. Then practice your new interview with a partner.**

EXTRA LISTENING AND SPEAKING ■ Interviewing a campaigner

I can discuss protest campaigns.

1 **Look at pictures A–C. What are the people campaigning about?**

2 2.42 **Listen to an interview. Which campaign in exercise 1 is the person supporting?**

3 2.42 **Study the key phrases. Then listen to the interview again and answer the questions.**

KEY PHRASES ■ Interviewing a campaigner

Why are you campaigning?
What does your sign say?
Can you explain how you feel about ... ?
What are you hoping to achieve?

1 In which city are the people protesting?
2 Approximately how many people are there in the park?
3 What time are the organizers going to speak?
4 Where is everyone going to march to?
5 What do they want the government to do?

4 **Answer the questions.**

1 What do people in your country campaign about?
2 What type of protest campaigns do you think are the most effective?
3 Have you ever campaigned for something?

5 2.43 **Listen. Then practice the dialogue with a partner.**

Reporter	Can you tell the listeners what you're doing?
Francesca	Yes, I'm joining in a march downtown.
Reporter	Why are you campaigning?
Francesca	Our local movie theater is going to close next month.
Reporter	Can you explain how you feel about that?
Francesca	I think it's unacceptable. If it closes, there won't be anything for teenagers to do here.
Reporter	What are you hoping to achieve?
Francesca	I hope the company will realize how we feel and that it won't close the theater.

6 ACTIVATE **Prepare answers to the questions in blue in exercise 5. Use one of the campaigns in exercise 1 or your own ideas. Then practice your new interview with a partner. Change roles.**

EXTRA LISTENING AND SPEAKING ■ Interviewing someone about a movie

I can talk about and recommend movies I have seen.

1 **Match the words in the box with the movies in posters A and B.**

love story   science fiction movie   vampire
alien   romantic   good special effects

2 3.09 **Listen to two interviews and check your answers to exercise 1.**

3 3.09 **Study the key phrases. Then listen to the interviews again. Answer questions 1–4 for each movie.**

KEY PHRASES ▢ Talking about movies

Which movie did you just see?
Who's in it?
What did you think of ... ?
Who would you recommend it to?
I'd recommend it to ... .

1 Who are the main actors?
2 Who are the main characters?
3 What did the viewer think of it?
4 Who would the viewer recommend it to?

4 3.10 **Listen to the sentences and number them in the order you hear them.**

a I watch it. ___
b I'll watch it. ___
c I've watched it. ___
d I'd watch it. ___
e I recommend it. ___
f I'll recommend it. ___
g I've recommended it. ___
h I'd recommend it. ___

5 3.11 **Look at poster C. Then listen and practice the dialogue.**

Interviewer Which movie did you just see?
Denise *Mamma Mia!* It's a musical.
Interviewer OK, and who's in it?
Denise Meryl Streep is one of the main actors. She plays a character named Donna.
Interviewer What did you think of the movie?
Denise The music was good, but the plot wasn't very believable.
Interviewer Who would you recommend it to?
Denise I'd recommend it to people who like Abba songs!

6 ACTIVATE **Change the words in blue in exercise 5 using information about a movie that you know. Then practice your new dialogue with a partner.**

EXTRA LISTENING AND SPEAKING ■ Discussing a picture

I can talk about a picture.

1 Match the words in the box with the definitions.

beautiful portrait strange
colorful traditional landscape
original art museum

1 a picture of the countryside
2 with a lot of color
3 pretty different from other things
4 a picture of a person
5 a place where paintings are exhibited
6 unusual and surprising
7 very lovely
8 not very modern

2 3.23 Listen to Rachel and Lewis. Which words in exercise 1 do you hear? Who says them?

3 3.23 Study the key phrases. Then listen again and answer the questions.

KEY PHRASES ○ Talking about a picture

What's it a picture of?
Who was it painted by?
Can you see the ... ?
at the top / bottom
on the right / left

1 Why is Rachel buying a present?
  a It's her birthday.
  b Her aunt has moved.
  c It's her aunt's birthday.
2 Who is the woman in the painting?
  a The artist, Frida Kahlo.
  b The artist's aunt.
  c A friend of the artist.
3 Which part of the picture does Rachel like the color of?
  a the leaves
  b the sky
  c the monkey
4 Why doesn't Lewis like the picture?
  a It isn't original.
  b It's sad.
  c It's happy.
5 What type of art does Rachel's aunt like?
  a unusual
  b pretty
  c traditional

Self-Portrait with Monkey

4 3.24 Listen. Then practice the dialogue. Find the picture in unit 8 that Rachel and Lewis are discussing.

Rachel What's it a picture of?
Lewis It's a picture of a beach with some strange watches on it.
Rachel Who was it painted by?
Lewis It says here it was painted by Salvador Dalí.
Rachel Can you see the cliffs on the right?
Lewis Oh, yes.
Rachel Well, I really like that, and I also like the yellow of the horizon in the background. What about you?
Lewis I'm not sure. I think it's a little depressing.

5 ACTIVATE Find another picture in unit 8 to discuss. Change the words in blue in exercise 4. Then practice your new dialogue with a partner.

CURRICULUM EXTRA ■ Technology: Television

I can talk about television technology in my country.

1 Check the meaning of the words in the box. Then match them with pictures A–F.

radio waves antenna binary code
satellite dish decoder interference

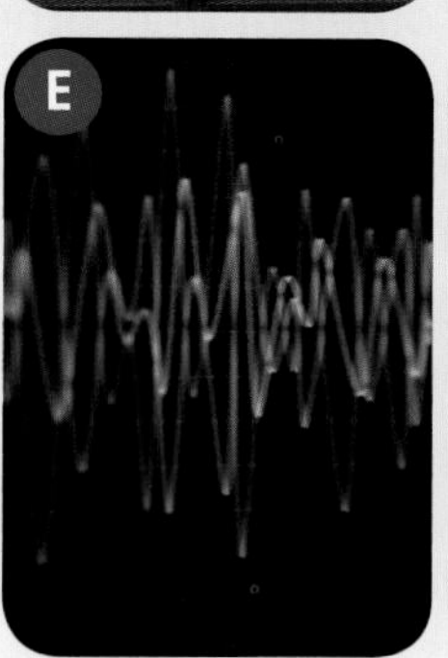

2 1.18 **Read and listen to the text. Are words and phrases 1–6 connected with analogue TV (A) or digital TV (D)?**

1 not many channels
2 not much interference
3 decoder
4 worse picture quality
5 radio waves
6 clear images

Broadcasting for the future

When television first started, the system of broadcasting was analogue. This meant that a TV antenna received radio waves from the TV companies. These transformed into sound and images on the TV screen. At the time, the system was revolutionary, but it wasn't perfect. It couldn't transmit many channels and the quality of the pictures was sometimes poor because of interference. For a long time, there was only analogue TV, but at the end of the 1990s, digital television arrived.

Digital TV doesn't use radio waves. Instead, it converts sound and images into binary code. This is a computer language which only consists of zeros and ones, and broadcasters can use it to send a lot of information very quickly. This digital information arrives at a TV via an antenna, a cable, a satellite dish, or broadband. Then a decoder converts the information back to sound and images. Decoders are either inside a TV or computer, or in a separate box which is connected to it.

Digital broadcasting is much better than the analogue system. There are a lot more channels because the TV companies can transmit much more information. The quality of the images and sound is much higher because there is less interference. Picture quality is even better on a high-definition TV (an HDTV) than on a standard TV, so viewers can enjoy movie theater-quality pictures in their own home.

3 Read the text again and answer the questions.

1 What type of broadcasting uses radio waves?
2 What problems were there with this system?
3 What is binary code?
4 How can TVs receive digital information? Name four routes.
5 Does a decoder have to be inside a TV? Explain your answer.
6 What's the difference between an HDTV and a standard TV?

4 Read the activities in 1–3. Compare the technology that was available in the past with the technology that is available now.

watching movies at home

In the past, people watched movies at home on video cassettes. After that, people mainly used DVDs. These days, people often watch movies online.

1 listening to music
2 communicating with friends
3 photography

5 ACTIVATE Answer the questions.

1 What type of TV is most common in your country, digital or analogue?
2 Where can you receive cable TV? What are the advantages of it?
3 What technology does your home have for receiving TV?
4 Which are more common in your area, antennas or satellite dishes?

CURRICULUM EXTRA ■ Geography: Sustainable development

I can write about an environmental problem.

1 **Check the meaning of the words in the box. Then complete the text.**

save	environment	community	facilities	solutions	recycles

2 1.35 **Read and listen to the text. Check your answers in exercise 1.**

Think globally, act locally

In 1992, the leaders of more than 100 countries met at the Earth Summit, a United Nations conference in Rio de Janeiro. They discussed issues which affect the [1]___, such as pollution and climate change, and talked about possible [2]___ to these problems. At this conference, they adopted a global strategy for "sustainable development." This means economic and social development which doesn't destroy the environment. One of the most important parts of their strategy is now called "Local Agenda 21."

The idea behind Local Agenda 21 (21 refers to the 21st century) is that if a lot of people do small things locally, then they can have a big impact nationally and an even bigger impact globally. For example, if one person decides to take the bus to work rather than drive a car, or always [3]___ his trash, it only makes a very small difference. However, if millions of people across the world do the same, the impact is huge. It's easy for every individual to do something small every day – at home, at school, or at work.

Local Agenda 21 encourages a collective responsibility towards the environment. For it to be effective, everyone in a [4]___ needs to work together. Local councils need to provide good [5]___, such as recycling and public transportation, and people need to use them. If everyone plays their part in a small way, they can both improve their local area and help to [6]___ the global environment.

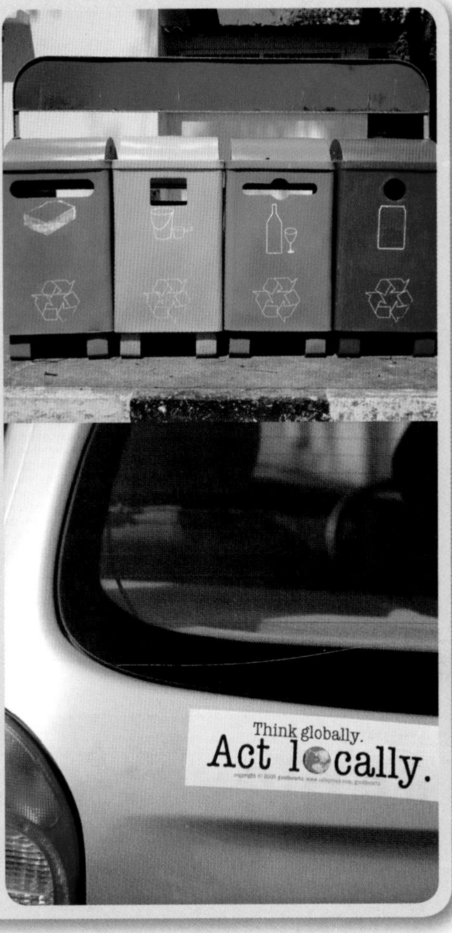
Think globally.
Act locally.

3 **Read the text again and write *true* or *false*. Correct the false sentences.**

1 Twenty-one people met at the Earth Summit.
2 Sustainable development means environmentally friendly development.
3 Using public transportation is better for the environment than driving.
4 It's difficult to contribute to Local Agenda 21.
5 Local Agenda 21 can only be successful if a lot of people help.
6 People don't need the help of local city councils.

4 **Think about things at your school that have a negative impact on the environment. What could you do to improve these things? Make a list of problems and solutions.**

Problems
A lot of students come to school by car. The cars pollute the air outside the school.
Solutions
Find out which students live near each other. Encourage them to come to school together in the same car.

5 **ACTIVATE** **Write a letter to your school magazine about one of the problems you listed in exercise 4. Include:**

- what the problem is
- why it is a problem
- what people / the school can do
- why this will help

CURRICULUM EXTRA ■ Technology: The Internet – wikis

I can write and edit wikis.

1 Check the meaning of the words in the box. Then complete the text below.

content   use   go live   double-check   update

2 2.04 **Read and listen to the text. Check your answers to exercise 1. Then match the headings 1–4 with paragraphs A–C. There is one heading that you do not need.**

1 What is Wikipedia?
2 Wiki – a free online encyclopedia
3 Wikipedia – advantages and disadvantages
4 What is a wiki?

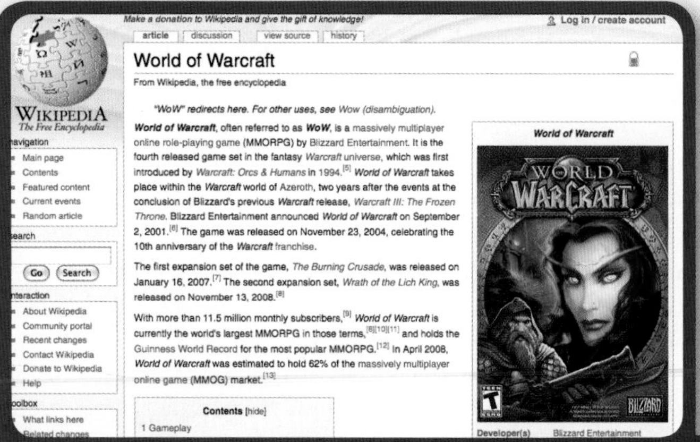

Make a donation to Wikipedia and give the gift of knowledge!

article | discussion | view source | history

Log in / create account

WIKIPEDIA
The Free Encyclopedia

navigation
- Main page
- Contents
- Featured content
- Current events
- Random article

search
Go Search

interaction
- About Wikipedia
- Community portal
- Recent changes
- Contact Wikipedia
- Donate to Wikipedia
- Help

toolbox
- What links here
- Related changes

World of Warcraft

From Wikipedia, the free encyclopedia

"WoW" redirects here. For other uses, see Wow (disambiguation).

World of Warcraft, often referred to as ***WoW***, is a massively multiplayer online role-playing game (MMORPG) by Blizzard Entertainment. It is the fourth released game set in the fantasy *Warcraft* universe, which was first introduced by *Warcraft: Orcs & Humans* in 1994.[5] *World of Warcraft* takes place within the *Warcraft* world of Azeroth, two years after the events at the conclusion of Blizzard's previous *Warcraft* release, *Warcraft III: The Frozen Throne*. Blizzard Entertainment announced *World of Warcraft* on September 2, 2001.[6] The game was released on November 23, 2004, celebrating the 10th anniversary of the *Warcraft* franchise.

The first expansion set of the game, *The Burning Crusade*, was released on January 16, 2007.[7] The second expansion set, *Wrath of the Lich King*, was released on November 13, 2008.[8]

With more than 11.5 million monthly subscribers,[9] *World of Warcraft* is currently the world's largest MMORPG in those terms,[8][10][11] and holds the Guinness World Record for the most popular MMORPG.[12] In April 2008, *World of Warcraft* was estimated to hold 62% of the massively multiplayer online game (MMOG) market.[13]

Contents [hide]
1 Gameplay

World of Warcraft

Developer(s) Blizzard Entertainment

3 Read the text again and answer the questions.

1 What's the origin of the word "wiki"?
2 What's Internet vandalism?
3 How was Nupedia different from Wikipedia?
4 What happened in 2001?
5 What advantages does Wikipedia have compared to a printed encyclopedia?
6 Why can the information on Wikipedia sometimes be inaccurate?

4 ACTIVATE Follow the instructions and create your own wiki.

1 Think of four interesting facts about one of the topics in the box. Then write a short text (wiki) about the topic.

your school   an online game   a celebrity   a social networking site   the Internet   a TV program

2 Exchange your wiki with a partner.
3 Read the wiki and make two changes. Remember you can add, delete, or edit facts.
4 Exchange your wikis again. Read your wiki and check that the language is correct.

An ever-changing document

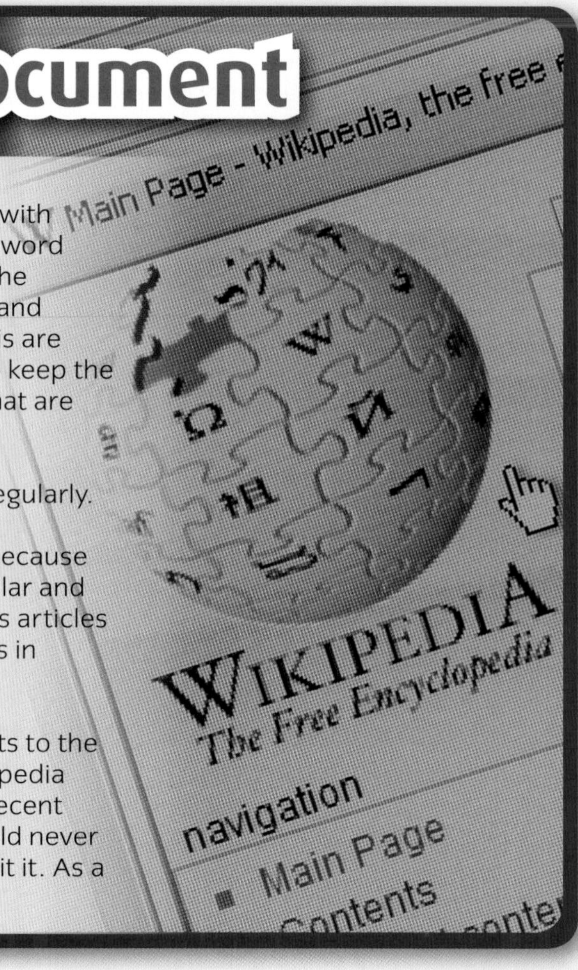

A ___
A wiki is a webpage that anyone can create on the Internet with simple software. The word "wiki" comes from the Hawaiian word for "quick." As soon as you've written a wiki, it can ¹___ on the web. Anyone who reads a wiki can click on "Edit this page" and then add, delete, or edit any of its ²___. This means that wikis are continually changing. Most of the changes are necessary to keep the information up to date, but Internet vandalism – changes that are wrong or offensive – can be a problem.

B ___
Wikipedia is familiar to most people who ³___ the Internet regularly. Wikipedia started in 2000 as part of Nupedia, a free, online encyclopedia written by experts. Wikipedia was different, because ordinary people wrote its content. It was immediately popular and became an independent website in 2001. Wikipedia now has articles in over 250 languages, including more than 4 million articles in English alone.

C ___
Wikipedia is growing bigger every day and there are no limits to the topics it covers. Because people ⁴___ wikis all the time, Wikipedia contains information about the very latest things, such as recent news events or advances in technology. However, you should never forget that Wikipedia is a wiki, and anyone can write and edit it. As a result, you should always ⁵___ facts before using them.

CURRICULUM EXTRA ■ Language and literature: Newspapers

I can talk about newspapers in my country.

1 Check the meaning of the words in blue. Then look at the newspapers in the pictures. What do you think is in each newspaper? Match phrases 1–10 with pictures A and B.

1 an interview with a pop star
2 articles about the economy
3 funny headlines
4 horoscopes
5 complex vocabulary
6 a review of an opera
7 an obituary
8 colloquial language
9 puzzles
10 celebrity gossip

2 2.18 Read and listen to the text. Check your answers in exercise 1.

3 Read the text again and write *true*, *false*, or *don't know*.

1 Newspapers aren't popular any more.
2 People buy more tabloids than quality papers.
3 It's more common to find articles about pop stars' lives in tabloids.
4 The language is very similar in both types of newspaper.
5 The same story can appear in both types of newspaper.
6 Quality newspapers don't contain articles about sports.

4 Answer the questions.

1 Do you read newspapers?
2 Which papers do you or people you know read?
3 How often do you or members of your family buy a newspaper?
4 Why do / don't you read a newspaper?

Read all about it!

These days, it's very easy to find out what's happening in the world. You can read or listen to the latest national and international news stories on your digital TV, tablet, or cell phone. However, a lot of people still prefer to get the news in a more traditional way, by reading a newspaper. In some countries, there are two distinct types of daily national newspaper – "quality" papers and tabloids. Both types inform and entertain, but they use different techniques to do this.

Quality newspapers

These are more serious than tabloids, both in their design and their content. They concentrate on more serious news topics, such as politics, economics, and international news. They use a formal style of language with longer sentences and technical vocabulary. As well as news, they often contain arts and culture reviews.

Tabloids

These concentrate on human interest stories and celebrity gossip. They often show large or controversial pictures of celebrities and politicians. They use shorter words and sentences, with colloquial words and expressions. Their headlines are large and sometimes funny. They usually contain features such as interviews, horoscopes, and problem pages.

Both types of newspaper share some characteristics. For example, most newspapers – quality and tabloids – contain articles about sports, weather forecasts, puzzles, and TV guides. When there's an important event such as an election or a natural disaster, it's usually on the front page of all newspapers.

5 ACTIVATE Write a list of newspapers in your country and answer the questions.

1 What type are they: quality, tabloid, or neither?
2 Which of the features in exercise 1 can you find in these newspapers?
3 Which newspaper do you like / dislike? Explain your answers.

CURRICULUM EXTRA ■ Citizenship: The school community

I can talk about students' rights and responsibilities.

1 Read the text. Match the headings a–e with paragraphs 1–5.

a Disruptive classes
b Mean behavior
c Prevention is better than cure
d A miniature community
e Punishments

2 2.31 **Listen to the text and check your answers in exercise 1.**

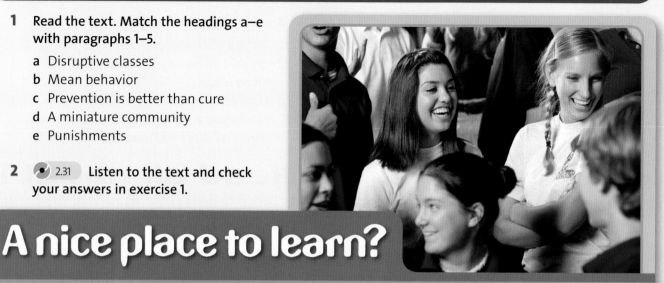

A nice place to learn?

1 ___
A school is like a small community. A local community should be a happy and safe place to live, and a school community should be a happy and safe place to learn. But like any community, sometimes there are problems.

2 ___
One of the most common problems at school is a lack of discipline in the classroom, for example, students chatting, using their cell phones, and generally not doing what the teacher wants. This type of behavior disrupts the class, and disturbs the teacher and the other students in the class who want to learn.

3 ___
Another common problem in schools is bullying. Bullying can be physical, verbal, or emotional. It can take the form of intimidation, insults, spreading rumors, or violence. These days, more girls are involved than boys, both as bullies and victims. Teachers may also be victims.

4 ___
When students break the rules, the school should have appropriate strategies to deal with the problem. Teachers can move students to a different place in the classroom to stop disruptions, or send students out of the classroom. For more serious problems, teachers can give detention, and in extreme cases, principals can suspend or expel students.

5 ___
The best solution, of course, is to prevent antisocial behavior before it happens. In some countries, students have citizenship lessons where they learn about their rights and responsibilities. Some schools also have a system of rewards for students so that they have a positive incentive to behave well.

3 Read the text again and answer the questions.

1 Is "a community" a good way to describe a school? Why / Why not?
2 Who suffers when someone causes problems in class?
3 Does bullying always involve violence? Explain your answer.
4 How can teachers discipline students who disrupt a class?
5 What punishments can schools use for more serious problems?
6 In which subject do students learn about appropriate behavior?

4 ACTIVATE Read the list and write *true* or *false*. Then think of more rights and responsibilities which are appropriate for your school.

Your rights and responsibilities in the classroom:

- To listen when the teacher is talking
- To try your best
- To send a text message when necessary
- To be polite
- To talk whenever you want
- To respect each other
- To have fun
- To cooperate
- To learn in a safe environment
- To distract others

CURRICULUM EXTRA ■ Geography: Natural environments

I can write about a coral reef.

1 Check the meaning of the words in the box. Then complete the text.

wildlife	mammals	layers	natural	vegetation	shrubs

2 2.44 Read and listen to the text. Check your answers in exercise 1.

3 Read paragraph 2 again. Label the diagram 1–4.

4 ACTIVATE Write two paragraphs about coral reefs. Use the notes below.

Paragraph 1 – Facts
What they are – underwater structures, tiny living animals
Distribution – cover 0.2% world's oceans
Location – warm shallow tropical oceans
Importance – habitat for over 1 million animal species

Paragraph 2 – Endangered
Already disappeared – nearly one third of coral reefs
Causes – pollution, climate change, scuba-diving, fishing, tourist souvenirs
Solutions – protection, not touching them

Tropical rainforests

Tropical rainforests are amazing places. You find them in Asia, Central and South America, and parts of Africa. The temperatures there are between 25 and 30°C all year round, and it rains heavily almost every day. These hot, wet conditions are ideal for plants, so the [1]___ is dense and rich, and the [2]___ is incredibly diverse. More than half of the world's plant and animal species live in these forests.

There are four [3]___ in a tropical rainforest. The top part is called the emergent layer. It consists of the tallest trees in the forest, which receive the most sunlight. The next section is called the canopy, and a huge number of birds, insects, reptiles, and [4]___ live there. There is so much food at this level that some animals never go down to the lower parts. The third section is called the understory. It's dark and cool, and consists of smaller trees and [5]___. The lowest part is called the forest floor. It's home to larger animals, like tapirs and jaguars. Only 1 percent of sunlight reaches the forest floor.

We've already destroyed more than half of the world's tropical rainforests, either for wood or through farming. If we carry on like this, we might wipe them out completely in less than forty years from now. One solution is to use the forests in a sustainable way, by using their [6]___ resources, such as fruit, nuts, and medicinal plants, without destroying the trees.

CURRICULUM EXTRA ■ Language and literature: Word building – nouns

I can form nouns using suffixes.

1 **Check the meaning of the words in the box. Then look at the picture and complete the text.**

thunder	softly	wavy	fools	pointed	chins

2 3.12 **Read and listen to the text. Check your answers in exercise 1.**

3 **Read the text again and choose the correct words to complete the summary.**

The Time Traveler has built a Time Machine and traveled [1]**back / forward** in time. He's met some people who all look [2]**the same / different**. He thinks they are [3]**attractive / ugly**. They seem [4]**friendly and cheerful / unfriendly and serious**, but the Time Traveler is surprised. He thought that people from the [5]**future / past** would be very [6]**stupid / intelligent**, but they aren't.

4 **Make nouns using the suffixes in the box. Then read the text again and check your answers.**

-ation	-ness	-ence	-ing	-ment

Verbs	Adjectives
1 mean	5 pretty
2 move	6 intelligent
3 converse	7 sad
4 feel	8 different

5 **Look at the texts on pages 96–101 and find verbs and adjectives. Then make nouns from these words using suffixes. Use a dictionary to help you. What other noun suffixes are there?**

wet – wetness

The Time Machine

by H.G. Wells

Looking closer at their faces, I saw some strange difference in their sweet prettiness. They all had the same [1]___ hair and this came to a sharp end at the neck and below the ears. There was none growing on their faces and their ears were very small. Their little [2]___ came to a point and their eyes were large and gentle.

Because they didn't try to speak to me, but simply stood smiling and speaking [3]___ to each other, I began the conversation. I pointed to the Time Machine and to myself. Then, after thinking for a moment how to describe time, I [4]___ to the sun. At once, a pretty little figure dressed in purple and white did the same and then made the sound of [5]___.

For a moment I was very surprised, though the meaning of his movement was clear enough. The question had come into my mind suddenly: were these people [6]___? I had always expected that people living about 800,000 years in the future would have much greater knowledge than us in science, art – everything.

But one of them had asked me a very simple question, which showed him to be on the level of intelligence of one of our five-year-old children. He had asked me, in fact, if I had come from the sun in a thunderstorm!

A feeling of sadness came into my mind. For a moment, I felt that I had built the Time Machine for no reason at all.

6 **ACTIVATE Complete the sentences with a noun. Use suffixes from exercise 4. Which suffixes do you use to form nouns in your language? Give examples.**

1 The ending spoiled my ___ of the book. (enjoy)
2 She felt a strange ___ as she walked into the empty house. (sense)
3 People had a difficult ___ during the war. (exist)
4 I could sense her ___. (happy)
5 I'd like to see a horror movie. Do you have any ___? (recommend)

CURRICULUM EXTRA ■ Visual arts: Art movements of the 20th century

I can describe an art movement.

1 Check the meaning of the words in the box. Which words would you use to describe which paintings?

bright bold colors　drips of paint
a comic strip　representative of real life
a brand name

2 3.25 **Read and listen to the text. Which art movements are the words in exercise 1 from?**

3 Read the text again. Write AE (Abstract Expressionism), PA (Pop Art), or N (Neither) for sentences 1–6.

1 It became popular during the Second World War.
2 It started in Europe.
3 Common objects appeared in the pictures.
4 The painting process itself was extremely important to the artists.
5 The artists were all the same nationality.
6 Famous people were sometimes portrayed.

4 3.26 **Look at the lines below and listen to part of an art class. Which line do the students think is the longest?**

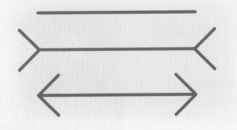

5 3.26 **Listen again and choose the correct words.**

1 Op Art means **Pop Art** / **Optical Art**.
2 Our brain makes us think that the **middle** / **bottom** line is the longest.
3 In fact, the lines are all **different lengths** / **the same length**.
4 Op artists **didn't like** / **copied** the art of the abstract expressionists.

6 ACTIVATE Write about the art movement Minimalism. Use the information in the box and your own ideas.

American　popular　1950s – 70s
extremely simple　shapes　no emotions
primary colors

20th century art

Abstract Expressionism

Abstract Expressionism is an art movement that became popular in the U.S. after World War II, from the mid 1940s to the end of the 1950s. The artists of this movement were also known as "The New York School." However, not all of them were American. Some were forced to move to the U.S. from Europe because of the war.

Abstract Expressionism was more of an attitude than a particular style. The characteristics of the paint itself and the act of painting were very important to its artists. Typically, broad brushes were used, and the paint was sometimes dripped or thrown onto a large canvas. The artists enjoyed this freedom of expression, and they depicted emotions in their paintings rather than actual objects.

Pop Art

Popular Art, or Pop Art, originated in Britain in the mid 1950s and became popular in the U.S. in the 1960s. It started as a reaction to Abstract Expressionism, which was considered too profound and pretentious by some people. "Pop artists" believed art should be simpler and more representative of real life. They wanted art to be more accessible to ordinary people.

Pop Art celebrated post-war materialism and consumerism. The images often depicted everyday objects, brand names, and packaging, such as tubes of toothpaste or boxes of cereal. Celebrities, the media, or comic strips also appeared. Bright, bold colors were used, and the pieces of art often contained the same image, repeated in different colors.

CULTURE ■ Television in the U.S.

I can make a survey about TV viewing habits.

1 1.19 **Complete the text with the numbers in the box. Then read, listen, and check your answers.**

8,000 9% 20,000 90 million
19% 66% 20 million

2 Read the text again and answer the questions.

1 What do you know about half of all homes in the U.S.?
2 How long does the average American watch TV for every day?
3 Which program always has the biggest TV audience?
4 What's special about the ads during the Super Bowl?
5 What do people do during "Mental Detox Week"?
6 What does a "TV-B-Gone" do?

3 YOUR CULTURE Answer the questions.

1 Do you or your friends have a TV in your bedroom?
2 How many hours a day do you watch TV? Do you think that is more or less than the average person in your country?
3 Which types of TV program are popular in your country?
4 Do you watch any American TV programs? Which ones?
5 Does TV cause any problems in your country? What problems?

4 TASK Work in groups. Write a survey of TV viewing habits in your class.

1 Work in pairs and prepare a questionnaire.
2 Look at the text for ideas.
3 Ask other students your questions and make notes.
4 Use your results to write a report.

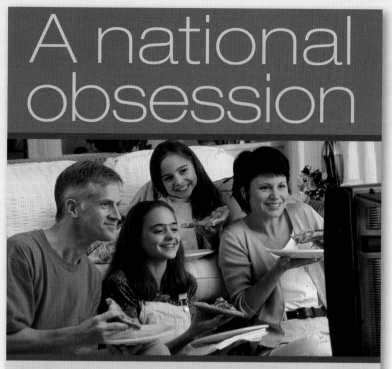

A national obsession

Some Americans watch a lot of television. There are more TVs than people in the typical American home today – only [1]___ of homes have just one TV, and half of all homes have three or more. Fifty percent of children between the ages of six and seventeen have a TV in their bedroom. The average person watches TV for about four and a half hours a day, and [2]___ of people regularly watch TV while they're having dinner. In fact, on average, Americans spend about [3]___ of their entire life watching TV!

The most popular types of TV programs in the U.S. are drama series, like *CSI*, and talent shows, like *American Idol*. However, every year, around [4]___ viewers also watch the Super Bowl, the most important football game of the year. This has the biggest TV audience of any show. Some companies spend a lot of money making creative and unusual ads especially for the Super Bowl, because they know that so many people will see them. Speaking of advertisements, the average American child watches over [5]___ ads a year!

All this TV can have negative effects. Americans see a lot of violence on their TV screens – the average child sees over [6]___ murders on TV before he or she even goes to high school. One organization, the Center for Screen-Time Awareness, is trying to change this. Every year, it encourages people to switch off their TVs for a whole week. This is called "Mental Detox Week." Some people even use a universal remote control called a "TV-B-Gone" to switch off televisions in public places. Mental Detox Week is becoming more and more popular every year – in 2008, [7]___ Americans took part.

CULTURE ■ Clean Up the World

I can plan an environmental event for where I live.

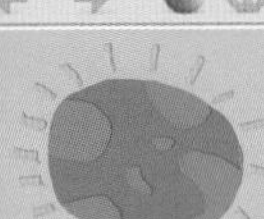

HOME ABOUT CONTACT FAQ JOIN SEARCH:

Clean Up the World

In 1987, Australian sailor Ian Kiernan competed in a round-the-world sailing race. He was so shocked and angry about the huge amount of trash that was polluting the world's oceans that he decided to do something about it.

Back home in Sydney, he organized Clean Up Sydney Harbour Day. Over 40,000 volunteers cleared away old cars, bottles, and plastic of all kinds. It was so successful that he started Clean Up Australia and then, in 1993, the Clean Up the World (CUW) project was born.

The organization's main annual event is Clean Up the World Weekend in September. During this weekend, over 600 groups from every continent clear waste from streets, beaches, river banks, and parks.

Around 35 million people in 120 countries now participate in the project and many volunteers continue their actions all year round, doing things like collecting and recycling waste, planting trees, and organizing exhibitions, competitions, and education events. If you want to organize a CUW project in your community, go to "Join" on the website and also read about other people's actions.

Clean Up the World actions

Volunteer divers from the Red Sea collected underwater trash while hundreds of local volunteers and tourists cleaned up the beaches. The divers continue their action all year by planting coral in the clean areas.

In Kenya, 200 students planted trees while 300 volunteers collected eight tons of waste. They sold a lot of this waste for recycling and made some money to help their community.

Click here to read more stories.

1 1.36 **Look at the pictures and answer the questions. Then read, listen, and check your answers.**

1. Who do you think the people are?
2. What are they doing?
3. Why do you think they are doing it?

2 Read the text again and answer the questions.

1. What shocked Ian Kiernan?
2. What was the first event that Kiernan organized?
3. When did Kiernan start Clean Up the World?
4. When does CUW Weekend take place?
5. What do the Red Sea divers do all year round?
6. What did Kenyan volunteers do with the trash they collected?

3 YOUR CULTURE Answer the questions.

1. What environmental organizations are there in your country?
2. What are their activities?
3. How do they raise money for their actions?
4. Have you ever taken part in an event to protect the environment? What did you do?
5. Would you take part in CUW Weekend? Why / Why not?

4 TASK Plan an event for a Clean Up the World Weekend in your area.

1. Work in groups of three or four, and choose an activity. Look at the ideas in the text and use your own ideas.
2. Decide what you want to achieve.
3. Plan your event. Think about:

   the time | getting volunteers | the place | getting media interest

4. Prepare a poster for your event.

CULTURE ■ Social networks around the world

I can do a survey on social networking.

1 2.05 **Look at the social networks in the pictures. Answer the questions for each site. Then read, listen, and check your answers.**

1 What can you do on these social networks?
2 Who do you think use them: teenagers, adults, or both?
3 Which social network do you think has the most users?

Social networks appeared in the U.S. in the late 1990s with sites like sixdegrees and Classmates, and with the arrival of Friendster in 2002, social networking really took off. A year later, the more serious LinkedIn arrived on the scene and immediately became popular with business people, and this is still true today.

However, it wasn't until the creation of MySpace in 2003, followed by Facebook in 2004, that social networking became enormous on every continent. Facebook's growth has been incredible and it has taken over as the world leader nearly everywhere. More recently, the microblogging site Twitter started in the U.S. in 2006, and its growth has also been amazing.

Who uses these networks and what are the national differences? With over one billion users worldwide, Facebook has become the leader in most countries. In Europe, it is the number one network in every country except Russia. In Italy, for instance, it grew from an unknown site to number one in only one year, pushing MySpace into second place!

The overall statistics don't show the whole picture because different networks appeal to different types of people. Research has shown that the average Facebook user is older and richer and more likely to be married than users of MySpace and Bebo, who are younger and more interested in having fun. Twitter users are also older and more interested in news, politics, and sports.

Nobody really knows what the future of these networks is. One interesting thing is that the number of Twitter users continues to grow every year. Other social networking sites like Pinterest and Google+ have attracted a lot of attention, too. Who knows what the next new thing will be?

2 Read the text again and answer the questions.

1 When and where did social networking start?
2 What type of people use LinkedIn?
3 In which European country is Facebook not the number one site?
4 What is the profile of the average Facebook user?
5 Which age group is more likely to use Bebo and MySpace?
6 What other sites have attacted lots of attention lately?

3 YOUR CULTURE Answer the questions.

1 Which social networking sites have you used / not used? Why / Why not?
2 What are the most popular social networks in your country?
3 What kind of information do people exchange on social networks?
4 Why do you think that social networking is popular?
5 What do you think are the dangers of social network sites?

4 TASK Make a survey on the social networks your friends use.

1 Work in pairs and prepare a short questionnaire. Use the ideas in the box and your own ideas.

networks they know | how often | networks they use | favorites | what they do

2 Interview other people and make notes of their answers.
3 Present your information in a bar graph and write a short summary of the results.

CULTURE ■ Teenage magazines

I can design a magazine.

1 2.19 **Look at the pictures of the magazines. Answer the questions for each magazine. Then read, listen, and check your answers.**

1 What do you think it's about?
2 Who do you think reads it: girls, boys, or both?
3 Would you like to read it?

2 Read the text again and answer the questions.

1 Which free gifts does Isabel mention?
2 What's good about the fashion pictures in *Seventeen*?
3 What type of magazines does Robbie mention?
4 Who does Robbie think *Top Gear* appeals to?
5 When did Anna start reading *Cool Scene*?
6 In what ways is the online magazine different?

Which magazines do you like reading?

If you go to a newsstand or supermarket in the U.S., you'll see a lot of magazines for teenagers. Most of them look quite similar – they have pictures of pop or TV stars on the cover and it's clear if they're for girls, boys, or both. Here, three teenagers tell us which are their favorite magazines and why.

I've just bought my favorite magazine, *Seventeen*. It's a really good deal because there's usually a free gift with it, like some makeup or jewelry. I love the fashion features about the latest styles. They're cool because they show normal girls in normal clothes, not really good-looking models in expensive designer clothes. There are also real-life stories and people's most embarrassing moments!

Isabel, 15

I don't think there are many magazines for teenage boys, except for a couple of sports magazines. My friend Josh buys a magazine about fitness and my brother buys one about computers, but they're more for adults than teenagers, I think. I love cars, and I buy *Top Gear* magazine every month. I think it appeals to adults and teenagers – my dad always wants to read my copy! This month, there's an article about Lewis Hamilton, and some pictures from this season's Formula 1 championship.

Robbie, 14

My brother and I have read *Cool Scene* magazine for about a year now. I love it because it has album reviews, concert dates, interviews with pop stars, and a lot of other things about music. There's lots of celebrity gossip in it, too, and things like personality quizzes and horoscopes. There's an online version of the magazine and I've read that, too. You can watch pop videos and listen to audio clips from interviews with celebrities. There are lots of good, new pictures there, too.

Anna, 15

3 YOUR CULTURE Answer the questions.

1 Do you often buy magazines? Why / Why not?
2 What type of things do you enjoy reading about in a magazine?
3 Do teenagers usually buy magazines in your country?
4 Which teenage magazines are there in your country?
5 Are there online versions of magazines that you read in your country?

4 TASK Design your ideal magazine.

1 Work in groups of three or four, and decide what type of magazine you are going to design.
2 List the features you want to put in the magazine. Look at the features in the text and use your own ideas.
3 Write a few articles for your magazine.
4 Write the contents page.
5 Present your magazine to the class.

CULTURE ■ Studying abroad

I can design a brochure about my school.

1 2.32 Look at the pictures. Can you guess the country? Then read, listen, and check your answer.

THE EXPERIENCE OF A LIFETIME

Spending a year in a foreign country has always been popular with college students, but now more high school students are also studying abroad, and one popular destination is New Zealand. We asked two teenagers why they chose New Zealand.

I spent last year at a coed public high school in Christchurch. I chose New Zealand because it is a beautiful and safe country and people speak English. I wasn't disappointed.

There were 1,400 students, including 50 foreigners, at my school. I was a little homesick at first because my English wasn't great, but I soon made a lot of friends and got used to the lifestyle. It's less stressful than here in Germany and people are more relaxed. The teachers were caring and my host family was really kind. Outdoor sports are big in New Zealand and I discovered a lot of new interests: sailing, mountaineering, and ... yes, rugby! You can't find better than New Zealand for a year abroad. It was the best decision I've ever made!

Dieter, 15, Germany

When I told my parents that I wanted to study abroad, they said OK, but it has to be a safe country with high educational standards. New Zealand was the obvious choice and now I don't want to go home to California! I go to a public girls' school in Auckland which has film studies as a special option. Since The Lord of the Rings, New Zealand's movie industry has become world famous, which is why I want to go to college here, too. But what I've enjoyed most are the free-thinking people and the stimulating discussions – I'm going to miss it.

Zoe, 14, U.S.

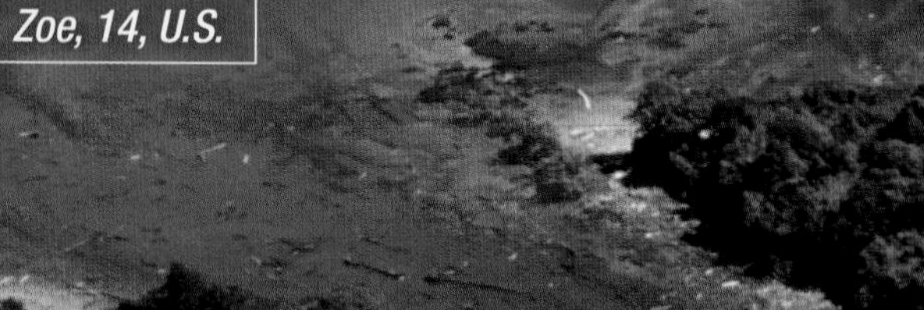

2 Read the text again and answer the questions.

1. Where do the students come from?
2. Which student hasn't left New Zealand yet?
3. Which student goes to a single-sex school?
4. Why did Dieter choose New Zealand?
5. How is the lifestyle different from Dieter's home country?
6. Why did Zoe choose New Zealand?
7. What is Zoe going to miss most?

3 YOUR CULTURE Answer the questions.

1. Would you like to study abroad? Why / Why not?
2. What country would you choose? Why?
3. Do college and high school students from your country study abroad?
4. What are popular destinations? Why?
5. Do foreign students study in schools and colleges in your country?

4 TASK Design a brochure about your school to attract foreign students.

1. Work in groups of three or four, and list positive things about your region, city, and school.
2. What special activities are there at your school or in your city?
3. Where could the students live?
4. Choose pictures to illustrate your brochure.
5. Present your brochure to the rest of the class.

CULTURE ■ Charities: Comic Relief

I can plan and present a funny competition or a game to raise money for charity.

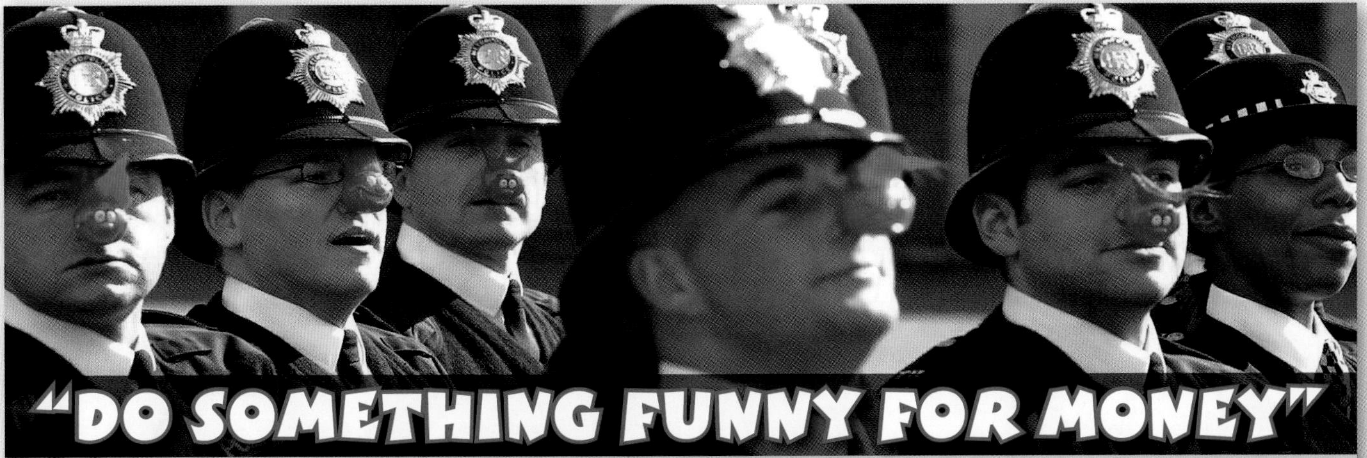

"DO SOMETHING FUNNY FOR MONEY"

Every two years on a Friday in March, you'll see a lot of strange things in streets, stores, offices, and schools all over the U.K. People might wear something unusual, some might have a crazy hairstyle, and others might do surprising things, like sit in a bath of baked beans for an hour. Some might simply wear a big, red nose. If you see anyone like this, you can donate some money. That's because it's Red Nose Day and these people want to "do something funny for money." Your donation will go to Comic Relief, the charity which organizes Red Nose Day.

Comic Relief started when a group of comedians decided to use comedy and humor to raise money to fight hunger, poverty, disease, and injustice, both in the U.K. and around the world. Red Nose Day raises millions of pounds each time it happens. There's a special TV program with comedy sketches that lasts all evening and it also reports on the people and projects that the money is going to help. Comic Relief usually spends 60 percent of the money on projects in Africa, and the rest in the U.K.

In the years that Red Nose Day doesn't happen, Comic Relief organizes another day of raising money, called Sport Relief. This time, all the events are connected to sport. One of them is the Sport Relief Mile. Thousands of members of the public, together with athletes and celebrities, ask their friends and family to sponsor them to run one, three, or six miles. If they don't want to run, they can walk – the most important thing is to finish and collect the money!

1 2.45 **Look at the pictures and answer the questions. Then read, listen, and check your answers.**

1 What are the people doing?
2 Why do you think they're doing it?

2 Read the text again and answer the questions.

1 How often does Red Nose Day take place?
2 Why do people do funny things on that day?
3 Who started Red Nose Day? Why?
4 How do TV viewers know who the money is going to help?
5 When does Sport Relief take place?
6 What do people do to raise money for Sport Relief?

3 YOUR CULTURE Answer the questions.

1 Have you ever done a sponsored event? What did you do?
2 Which charities are there in your country?
3 Who / What do they help?
4 How do people raise money for charity in your country?
5 How do celebrities help to raise money in your country?

4 TASK Plan a funny competition, game, or quiz to raise money for Red Nose Day. Present your idea to the class.

1 Work in groups of three or four, and decide what you are going to do. Remember, your idea should be funny.
2 Make notes about your event. Decide:
   - what you are doing exactly
   - what the rules are
   - who can take part
   - how you intend to raise money
3 Present your idea to the rest of the class.
4 Have a class vote for the best idea.

CULTURE ■ The British movie industry

I can perform a scene from a famous movie.

1 3.13 **Complete the text with the numbers in the box. Then read, listen, and check your answers.**

5,481 2 1936 22 41

LIGHTS, CAMERA, ACTION!

The British movie industry isn't the biggest in the world. For example, Hollywood in the U.S. and Bollywood in India both produce more movies. However, if you consider the international success of its movies and the talent of its actors, it's definitely one of the best. With directors like David Yates, who worked on some of the Harry Potter movies, and actors like Christian Bale, who played Batman in *The Dark Knight*, the British movie industry has a fantastic reputation around the world.

Pinewood Studios, near London, is the home of the British movie industry, and British and international filmmakers have made movies there since [1]___. It's possible to film all types of scenes at Pinewood, as its facilities are some of the best in the world. As well as [2]___ stages, it has underwater tanks, beautiful gardens, enormous old country houses, and even its own forest. Pinewood is home to the biggest stage in Europe, the "007 Stage," which measures [3]___ m^2. It's been the setting for an underwater shipwreck, the Louvre museum, a chocolate river, a square in Venice, and an entire fishing village.

One of the most popular series in the history of British movies is the James Bond series. It's the longest-running series. There have been [4]___ Bond movies so far, starting with *Dr. No* in 1962. Daniel Craig is the sixth actor to play the world's most famous spy and Bond's popularity continues. The combination of explosions, cool cars, and saving the world seems to be successful; apparently more than [5]___ billion people, or nearly one in three in the entire world, have seen a Bond movie.

2 Read the text again and answer the questions.

1. Which two countries in the text have bigger movie industries than Britain?
2. What's Christian Bale famous for?
3. What happens at Pinewood Studios?
4. What's the biggest stage in Europe called?
5. When was the first James Bond movie?
6. Why are James Bond movies popular, according to the text?

3 YOUR CULTURE Answer the questions.

1. Who are the most famous actors from your country?
2. Does your country have an important movie industry?
3. Which movies from your country have been popular around the world?
4. Are the Harry Potter and James Bond movies popular in your country? Why / Why not?
5. Which movies from other countries are popular in your country?

4 TASK Prepare and perform a scene from a famous movie.

1. Work in groups of three or four.
2. Choose a movie that everyone knows, for example: *Star Wars*, *Titanic*, *Avatar*, *Twilight*.
3. Choose a short scene from the movie to act out to the class. Decide which character each person plays.
4. Write each actor's text.
5. Present the scene to the class.

CULTURE ■ Graffiti artists – past and present

I can plan a mural.

B

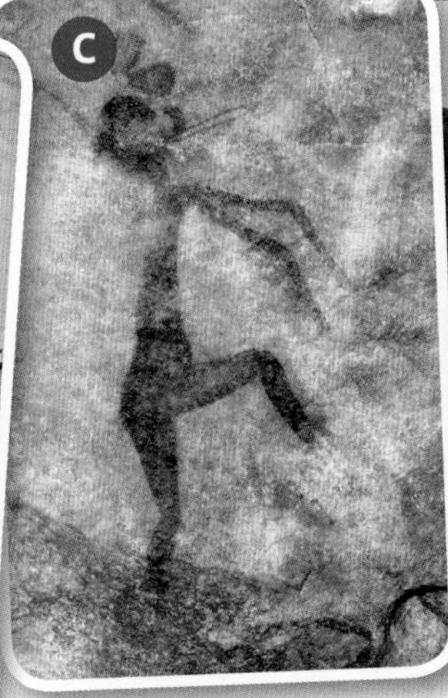

C

D

1 3.27 **Look at the pictures A–D and answer the questions. Then read, listen, and check your answers. Which picture is not mentioned in the text?**

1 How old are these paintings?
2 Where can you find these paintings?
3 Who painted them?
4 Which painting do you like best?

From rock art to urban graffiti

Prehistoric rock art isn't a hot topic with art historians because it isn't considered to be an art movement like Impressionism or Surrealism. But how different is this art from contemporary art forms like urban graffiti and mural paintings?

Prehistoric artists represented their world and beliefs with visual images which they carved or painted on cave walls. Some of these paintings, like the Bradshaw paintings in northern Australia, are incredibly beautiful. There are over 100,000 Bradshaw paintings and they may be nearly 50,000 years old; nobody really knows. These ancient artists used natural paints and made paint brushes from sticks, rocks, and animal fur to create these unique works of art. The Bradshaws are very special because, instead of showing wild animals like 30,000-year-old European cave paintings, they show humans with decorated hair and clothes. One painting of a beautiful dancer is certainly as great as any modern painting. We will never really know why these pictures were painted, but it is quite possible that the artist just wanted to create something beautiful.

The same is true for the graffiti art movement which has developed recently in the U.S. and other parts of the world. Graffiti artists paint on walls and old buildings, so it isn't very different from rock art. Of course, a lot of graffiti is not art, but some of these paintings are true works of art which improve the gray urban landscape and transform dirty old walls into beautiful murals. The Brazilian street artists, Otavio and Gustavo Pandolfo (Os Gêmeos), are among the most famous graffiti artists in the world. They create amusing or shocking street pictures to represent their ideas and comment on social and political situations.

Like ancient rock art, modern graffiti art decorates the environment and shows the artists' world and beliefs.

2 **Read the text again and answer the questions.**

1 What did prehistoric artists paint?
2 How are the Bradshaw paintings different from European cave art?
3 What did the ancient artists paint with?
4 Why was ancient rock art created?
5 How is urban graffiti similar to ancient rock art?
6 How are Os Gêmeos similar to ancient rock artists?

3 YOUR CULTURE **Answer the questions.**

1 What great / terrible graffiti have you seen?
2 How do you feel about graffiti? Does it improve the urban landscape?
3 What ancient art is there in your country?
4 Who were the artists?
5 How much graffiti is there in your city? Is it art?
6 Look at the mural in picture D. What is special about this painting?

4 TASK **You are going to plan a mural for an ugly wall or building in your city and write a letter to the city council about your idea.**

1 Work in pairs and choose a place for your mural.
2 Decide what the picture will be like.
3 What will it hide or decorate?
4 What will it show?
5 Will it be funny / shocking / beautiful?
6 How big will it be?
7 Write a letter to the city council presenting your idea. (Look at page 65 for a formal letter model.)
8 Present your idea to the class.
9 Have a class vote for the best idea.

Build your vocabulary: regular and irregular verbs

1 Find the simple past forms. Complete the table.

w r o t e a r g u e d h a
d d r o v e c r i e d s h o
u t e d r e c o r d e d f e
l t c o p i e d t h o u g h
t w e n t h i d h e a r d
k n e w b o u g h t f o u
n d d i d b e c a m e s p
o k e c h a t t e d l a u
g h e d s p e n t l i v e d

Regular verbs	Irregular verbs	
argue *argued*	write *wrote*	8 have
1 chat	1 become	9 hear
2 copy	2 buy	10 hide
3 cry	3 do	11 know
4 laugh	4 drive	12 speak
5 live	5 feel	13 spend
6 record	6 find	14 think
7 shout	7 go	15 write

2 Complete the story. Use some of the simple past verbs from the table in exercise 1.

Love u 4ever

I recorded an American sitcom on Channel 4 last week. It was really funny. I *laughed* so much that I [1]c___! It was called *Love u 4ever* and it was about a lazy husband and his horrible wife.

They [2]a___ about everything all the time. He [3]s___ all day watching TV and she [4]s___ at him because he never went out. One day he [5]d___ to the mall and he [6]b___ a portable TV.

He [7]w___ home and he [8]h___ in the back yard with the TV. The wife [9]h___ the TV. When she [10]f___ her husband in the back yard, she [11]f___ very angry.

Extend your vocabulary: TV and DVDs

3 Match the verbs in the box with the buttons on the remote control.

change channel eject fast forward
pause play record rewind ~~turn on / turn off~~

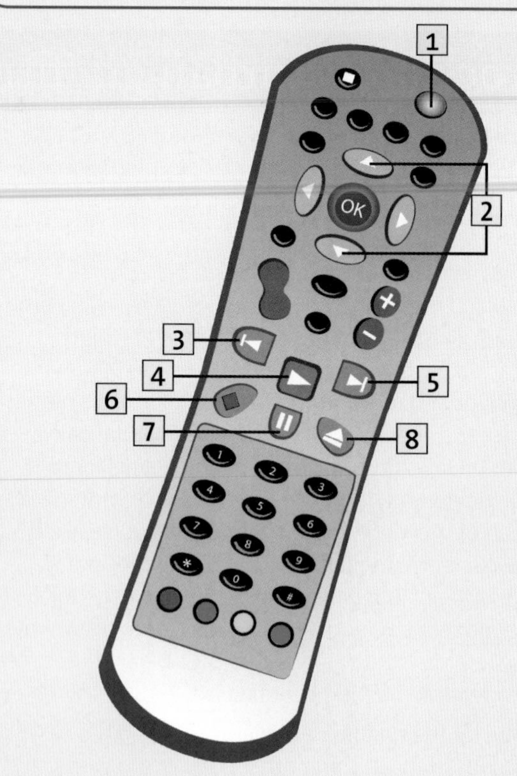

1 *turn on / turn off*

VOCABULARY BANK ■ Compound nouns • Waste

Build your vocabulary: compound nouns

1 Make seven more compound nouns with words from A and B.

A
~~art~~
shopping
water chocolate
pencil tennis
video
paper

B
cake
clip bottle
case basket
camera
racket
~~gallery~~

1 *art gallery*

2 Label the pictures. Use compound nouns.

1 *bus stop*

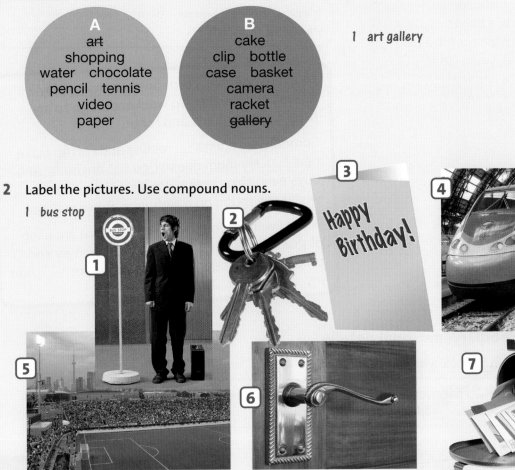

Extend your vocabulary: waste

3 Label the pictures with the words in the box.

trash can   waste basket   ~~collection center~~   landfill site
trash barrels   dumpster   recycling center   trash bag

collection center

1 ____________

2 ____________

3 ____________

4 ____________

5 ____________

6 ____________

7 ____________

VOCABULARY BANK ■ Verb and noun collocations • Personal details

Build your vocabulary: verb and noun collocations

1 Match verbs 1–6 with nouns a–f.

1 make	a shopping
2 score	b a band
3 go	c points (on a test)
4 join	d your English
5 improve	e money
6 spend	f friends

2 Complete the text with the words in the box.

friends hours ~~laptop~~ points rock group shopping English

Like most people, I turn on my *laptop* to play as well as to study. On weekends, I go to my favorite chat rooms and I chat.

Sometimes I spend [1]___ online and I often make new [2]___. My mom doesn't go [3]___ anymore. She buys everything online. My sister has joined a [4]___ which she found on a webpage at her college!

When I want to improve my [5]___, there are a lot of great websites with vocabulary games and practice exercises. I usually score more [6]___ than my sister!

Extend your vocabulary: personal details

3 Match the words in the box with the picture.

country nickname password ~~first name(s)~~ zip code e-mail address last name(s) city, state address / street

1 *first name (s)*

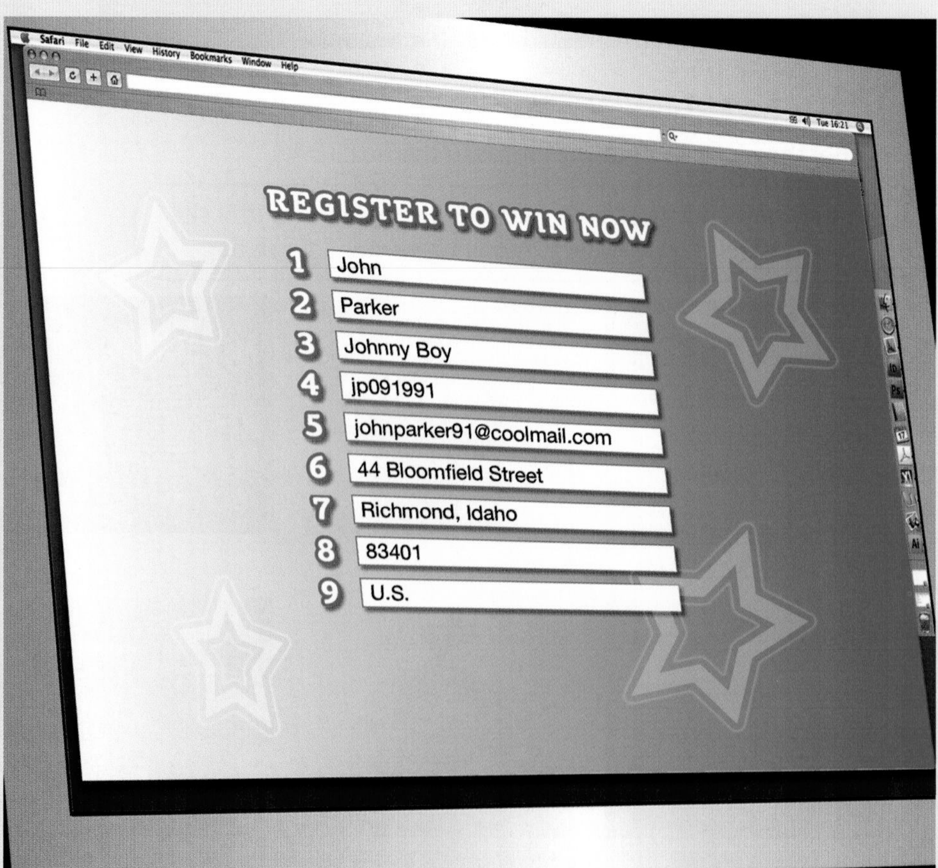

REGISTER TO WIN NOW
1 John
2 Parker
3 Johnny Boy
4 jp091991
5 johnparker91@coolmail.com
6 44 Bloomfield Street
7 Richmond, Idaho
8 83401
9 U.S.

VOCABULARY BANK ■ Prefixes and suffixes • Music

Build your vocabulary: prefixes and suffixes

1 Choose the correct suffix or prefix.

~~un-~~ -ful -less -able un- -less -able -ful un-

healthy *unhealthy*
1 peace ______
2 friendly ______
3 understand ______
4 home ______
5 wonder ______
6 happy ______
7 child ______
8 notice ______

2 Add prefixes and suffixes to the words in the box. Then use the words to complete the sentences.

~~sense~~ break usual life lucky end spite play drink

Why did the interviewer ask all those stupid questions? It was really *senseless*.
1 That new Hollywood movie was five hours long. It was ___!
2 Our dog loves running after his ball. He's very ___.
3 Be careful with this box. There are a lot of ___ things in it.
4 I like that band's new album. It's really ___ and very different to other pop music.
5 "Do you think the tap water in this hotel is OK?" "Yes, it's ___."
6 After the cat fell off the roof, it was completely ___, but then it started moving again.
7 That singer has been number two on the charts for weeks. He's never been to number one – he's very ___.
8 The journalists wrote some horrible and ___ things about my favorite actor's new haircut.

Extend your vocabulary: music

3 Match the words in the box with the pictures.

~~keyboard~~ recording studio amplifier bass guitar drums microphone speakers trumpet

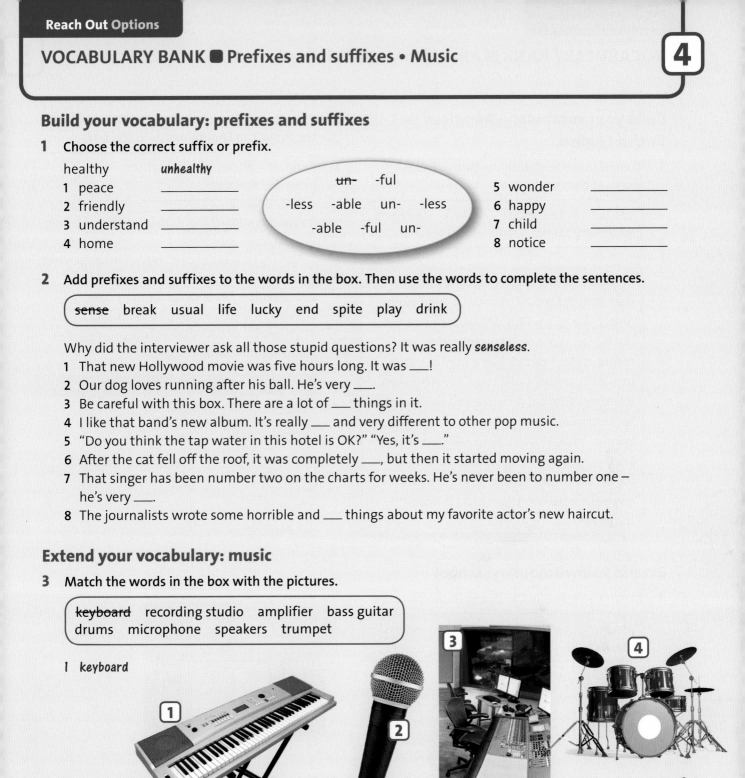

1 *keyboard*

VOCABULARY BANK ■ American vs. British English • School

Build your vocabulary: American vs. British English

1 **Complete the text with the British English words in the box.**

petrol mobile phone rubbish trousers ~~secondary school~~ road head teacher

I had a terrible day yesterday! First, I was late for *secondary school*. I was riding along the [1]___ when my motorcycle ran out of [2]___. I started to walk with my motorcycle. I didn't have my [3]___ with me, so I couldn't call the [4]___. After ten minutes, I found a café and I parked the motorcycle. I decided to run because I was so late. When I was nearly there, I fell over. I was OK, but there was a lot of [5]___ in the street. My [6]___ were covered with food and dirt. It was horrible!

2 **Read the sentences. Complete the table with the American English words in the box.**

cookie chips movie soccer ~~candy~~ sneakers

A sweet is something with a lot of sugar that you can eat.

1 You fry thin slices of potatoes in oil to make crisps.
2 A biscuit is like a small crunchy cake.
3 You can watch a film on a DVD.
4 We play football after school.
5 I'm wearing trainers today.

British English	American English
sweet	*candy*
crisps	[1]___
biscuit	[2]___
film	[3]___
football	[4]___
trainers	[5]___

Extend your vocabulary: school

3 **Match the words in the box with the pictures.**

assembly bike racks cafeteria lockers playground ~~school gates~~

1 *school gates*

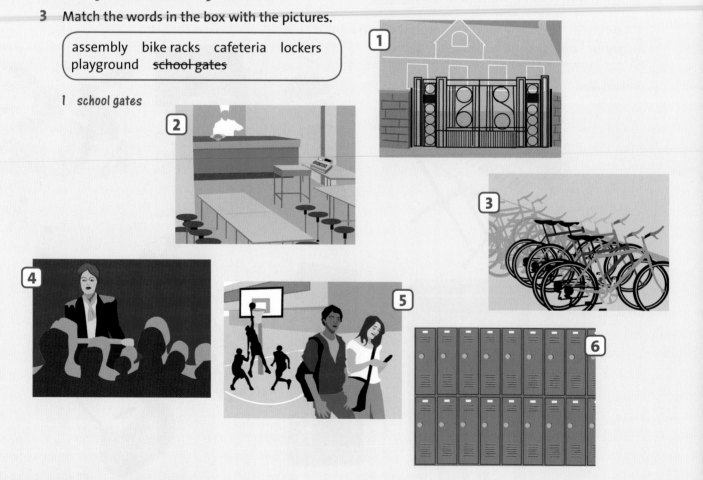

VOCABULARY BANK ■ Negative prefixes: *un-*, *im-*, and *in-* • The environment 6

Build your vocabulary: negative prefixes: *un-*, *im-*, and *in-*

1 Look at the words in bold. Write new words with *un-*, *im-*, or *in-*.

That woman is awful. She's really ~~friendly~~.
unfriendly

1. This map of my hometown isn't correct. It's very **accurate**. ___
2. They're **dependent**. They always work well on their own. ___
3. It isn't a good idea to have elephants in the circus. It's **moral**. ___
4. You don't see many white tigers in the wild. They're pretty **usual**. ___
5. He's very **polite**. He never says thank you to people. ___
6. She eats a lot of very **healthy** food like candy and French fries. ___

2 Match the prefixes to the words. Then use the words to complete the sentences.

un-	in-	im-	un-	in-	im-
un-	in-	im-			

___mature	___expensive	___safe
___common	___visible	___modest
___tolerant	___friendly	___patient

Don't climb the walls of that old building! They're *unsafe*.

1. Jake is ___ in class. He always behaves like a small child.
2. Those MP3 players don't cost very much. They're pretty ___.
3. I'm a very ___ person. I hate waiting a long time for the bus.
4. You don't see many of those birds here. They're pretty ___.
5. Rebecca always says that she's really good at tennis. She's very ___.
6. We can't see those very small creatures. They're ___ to the human eye.
7. He's very ___. He never listens to or accepts other people's ideas.
8. They're incredibly ___. Why don't they smile and say hello?

Extend your vocabulary: the environment

3 Match the words in the box with the pictures.

~~deforestation~~ global warming
flood drought ice caps
endangered species

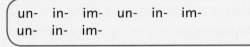

1 *deforestation*

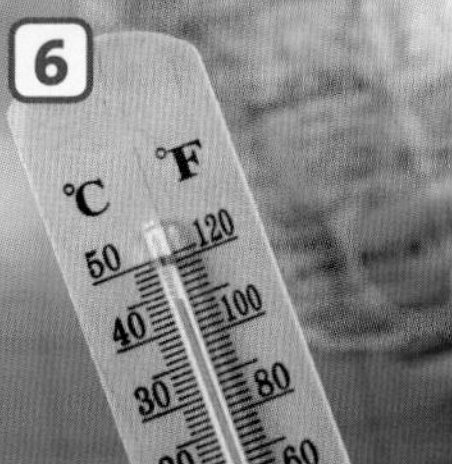

VOCABULARY BANK ■ Suffixes: *-er* and *-or* • Filmmaking

Build your vocabulary: suffixes *-er* and *-or*

1 Write the verbs in the box in the correct list.

~~act~~ speak view conduct edit paint create direct produce

-er

-or
actor

2 Complete the sentences with nouns from the table in exercise 1.

The **director** is telling the actors something important. Please be quiet.

1 How many people watched the new drama on HBO? There were 2.3 million ___.
2 Who wrote the first episode of *The Simpsons*? Matt Groening was the ___ of *The Simpsons*.
3 This picture is beautiful. I think the ___ was Mexican.
4 How can we connect these two scenes? The ___ will add some special effects.
5 Is John in the orchestra? No, he leads the orchestra. He's the ___.
6 There were a lot of interesting ___ at the meeting.

Extend your vocabulary: filmmaking

3 Match the words in the box with the pictures.

costume designer ~~camera operator~~ extras makeup artist movie producer sound engineer

1 camera operator

VOCABULARY BANK ■ Synonyms • Works of art

Build your vocabulary: synonyms

1 Match words 1–8 with synonyms a–h.

1 rich	a assist
2 buy	b huge
3 students	c wealthy
4 try	d pupils
5 living room	e attempt
6 help	f glad
7 enormous	g purchase
8 happy	h lounge

2 Use words a–h from exercise 1 to complete the sentences.

That artist earns a lot of money and she's very *wealthy*.

1 Did you see that big tiger at the zoo? It was ___!
2 There are at least thirty ___ in every class.
3 I know the last question is difficult, but please ___ to answer it.
4 They were very ___ when they bought the beautiful painting at the auction.
5 We often ___ tickets for exhibitions on the Internet. It's much easier.
6 My glasses aren't in the kitchen. Perhaps they're in the ___.
7 I sometimes ___ my father with his work.

Extend your vocabulary: works of art

3 Match the words in the box with the pictures.

statue	vase	~~mosaic~~	mural	still life
stained-glass window	frame	tapestry		

1 *mosaic*

OXFORD
UNIVERSITY PRESS

Great Clarendon Street, Oxford, OX2 6DP, United Kingdom

Oxford University Press is a department of the University of Oxford. It furthers the University's objective of excellence in research, scholarship, and education by publishing worldwide. Oxford is a registered trade mark of Oxford University Press in the UK and in certain other countries

First published in 2014
2018 2017 2016 2015 2014
10 9 8 7 6 5 4 3 2

ISBN: 978 0 19 485324 8

Printed in China

This book is printed on paper from certified and well-managed sources.

ACKNOWLEDGMENTS

The publisher would like to thank the following for permission to reproduce photographs and video footage: Alamy Images; Amnesty; CERN; Corbis; Getty Images; Google; MK2; NASA; Photolibrary; POST; Rex Features; The United Nations; The Wellcome Trust; Zooid.

The authors and publisher are grateful to those who have given permission to reproduce the following extract of copyright material: p.102 Extract from Penguin Reader *The Time Machine* by H. G. Wells, retold by David Maule, adapted from the original title by H. G. Wells. Reproduced by permission of United Agents on behalf of: The Literary Executors of the Estate of H. G. Wells, and Pearson Education Ltd.

The publisher and authors would like to thank the following teachers for their contribution to the development of this course: Romaine Ançay, Ursula Bader, Dominique Baillifard, Kinga Belley, Jaantje Bodt, Michel Bonvin, Coralie Clerc, Teresita Curbelo, Yvona Dolezalova, Lukas Drbout, Pierre Filliez, Olga Forstova, Christelle Fraix, Attie van Grieken, Roger Grunblatt, Cagr Gungormui, Christoph Handschin, Joe Hediger, Jana Vackova Hezinova, Maria Higina, Jaroslava Juzkova, Martin Kadlec, Urs Kalberer, Lena Kigouk, Joy Kocher, Murat Kotan, Marcela Kovarova, Jitka Kreminova, Lucie Machackova, Doubravka Matulova, Jitka Melounkova, Dana Mikesova, Noemi Nikolics, Sabrina Ragno, Denis Richon, Sonja Rijkse, Susanna Schwab, Dagmar Simkova, Jana Simkova, Nuria Smyth, Lenka Spackova, Rita Steiner, Anne-Marie Studer, Milan Svoboda, Anneli Terre-Blanche, Maria Cecilia Verga, Marta Vergara, Donna Van Wely.

The publisher and authors would like to extend special thanks to Ursula Schaer *for sharing her insights and for her contribution to the course.*

The publisher and authors would like to thank Sue Sileci *for her valuable work in developing* Reach Out.

Illustrations by: Paul Daviz pp.14, 32, 34; Mark Duffin p.69; Stephen Dumayne/Meiklejohn p.23; KJA p.106; Peter Kyprianou/Illustration Ltd pp.39; David Oakley/Arnos Design Ltd p.112, 114; Andy Parker p.102.

Commissioned photography by: Chris King pp.24, 34, 44, 54, 64, 74, 84.

Cover photographs: Getty Images (Teens climbing rock/Ligia Botero/Photonica), iStockphoto (Teens doing homework outdoors/Bart Coenders), Photolibrary (School students with globe/Image Source), (Teens reading a map/Paul Viant & Carrie Beecroft/White).

The publisher would like to thank the following for their permission to reproduce photographs: Action Plus p.92 (Playing hockey/ Glyn Kirk); Alamy Images pp.6 (teen shopping/amana images inc.), 7 (teen couple/Image Source), 17 (interview/D. Hurst), 17 (satellite image/Marshall Ikonography), 25 (Litter on beach/John Cole), 27 (festival stage/epa european pressphoto agency b.v.), 33 (computer user/Angela Hampton Picture Library), 45 (AlamyCelebrity), 48 (classroom/Malcolm Case-Green), 52 (boy red top/MBI), (boy curly hair/Picture Partners), 60 (carrots/Alistair Scott), 61 (food boxes/Jim West), 67 (crowded classroom/David Grossman), 87 (Reichstag Building/Christo/Picturebank), 89 (A box of aspirin/Steve Stock), 90 (cnn/IanDagnall Laptop Computing), 92 (students blue tshirt/Bob Daemmrich), 92 (Crowded classroom/Rob Few), 96 (TV aerial/Luxio), 96 (Digital receiver box/David J. Green - studio), 98 (Wikipedia website/Gary Lucken), 99 (New York Times/Richard Levine), 101 (Rainforest/Images & Stories), 106 (Facebook logo/Eddie Gerald), (Myspace logo/NetPics), (Twitter logo/PSL Images), (Bebo logo/Alex Segre), (Linkedin logo/Alex Segre), 107 (car magazine), 108 (bungee jumper/ IML Image Group Ltd), 111 (graffiti B/imagebroker), 113 (mailbox 7/Judith Collins), 118 (microphone boom man/Image Source), 119 (stained glass/David R. Frazier Photolibrary Inc.), (mural/Marion Kaplan); Albright Knox Art Gallery p.95 (Self-Portrait with Monkey 1938, (oil on masonite) © 2009, Banco de Mexico Diego Rivera & Frida Kahlo Museums Trust, Mexico D.F./DACS; Arnos Design Ltd pp.18 (Can of fizzy drink), 18 (Bottle of shampoo), 18 (Washing powder), 18 (Bag of apples), 18 (Bar of chocolate), 18 (Toothpaste), 72 (books), 73 (Book cover of The Invisible Man), 73 (Twilight book cover), 75 (Books), 89 (Batteries), 89 (Light bulbs), 90 (Collage of websites), 97 (Think Globally car sticker), 98 (Wikipedia page); BBC Photolibrary pp.89 (batteries, light bulbs), 97 (sticker), 99 (newspapers), 113 (birthday card), 116; Bradshaw Foundation, Geneva pp.111 (dancers); Bridgeman Art Library Ltd pp.78 (The Drachenfels, Germany, c.1823-24 (w/c & bodycolour with scraping out over pencil on paper), Turner, Joseph Mallord William (1775-1851)/ Manchester Art Gallery, UK), 78 (Mulberry Tree, 1889 (oil on canvas), Gogh, Vincent van (1853-90)/Norton Simon Collection, Pasadena, CA, USA), 79 (Mona Lisa, c.1503-6 (oil on panel) by Vinci, Leonardo da (1452-1519) Louvre, Paris, France/Giraudon), 80 (Bicycle Wheel, 1963 (mixed media), Duchamp, Marcel (1887-1968)/Private Collection/© DACS), 81 (L.H.O.O.Q, 1919 (colour litho), Duchamp, Marcel (1887-1968)/Private Collection/© DACS/Cameraphoto Arte Venezia), 81 (Fountain, 1917/64 (ceramic), Duchamp, Marcel (1887-1968)/The Israel Museum, Jerusalem, Israel/© DACS/Vera & Arturo Schwarz Collection of Dada and Surrealist Art), 84 (Maya with a Doll, 1939 (oil on Canvas) © Succession Picasso/DACS London 2010/Musee Picasso, Paris, France), (Compression n.1955 (mixed media)/Cesar Baldaccini © DACS 2010), 84 & 86 (The Scream/The Munch Museum/The Munch-Ellingsen Group), 85 (The Persistence of Memory, 1931 (oil on canvas, Dali, Salvador (1904-89)/Museum of Modern Art, New York, USA/© DACS), 103 (In the Car, 1963 (magna on canvas), Lichtenstein, Roy (1923-97)/Scottish National Gallery of Modern Art, Edinburgh, UK/© DACS), 103 (Spike's Folly II, 1960 (oil on canvas), Kooning, Willem de (1904-97)/Private Collection/© DACS); Camera Press Ltd p.11 (Reality Cats/ED SY); John Clem Clarke p.103 (Cola Billboard with kind permission from Trillion Clarke); CBS p.10 (Kids Nation/ CBS/Cornelia Schnall); Corbis pp.4 (Neptune/Denis Scott), 4 (Sperm whale/Denis Scott/Comet), 4 (vintage TV family/ Camerique/ClassicStock), 19 (toilet rolls/Bloomimage), 26 (market/Image Source), 28 (ball of wires/Images.com), 29 (webcam/Images.com), 37 (BMX down ramp/Thomas Fricke), 37 (Man on BMX bike/Daniel Attia), 37 (BMX rider on ramp/Thomas Fricke), 47 (Taylor Lautner/Frank Trapper), 55 (Student by school lockers/Kelly Redinger/ Design Pics), 62 (deforestation/Mast Irham/epa), 63 (protesters/G. Brad. Lewis), 67 (two boys/Paul Seheult/ Eye Ubiquitous/Co), 70 (People watching 3D film), 77 (loe Saldana/Stephanie Reix), 82 (Guggengeim/Eberhard Streichan/lefa), 83 (Guggenheim museum/Eberhard Streichan), 95 (Self Portrait with Monkey by Frida Kahlo/ Albright-Knox Art Gallery), 100 (Teenagers/Tim Pannell/ Flirt), 104 (American Super Bowl/Wally McNamee), 104 (family/John Henley), 108 (rugby/Anthony Phelps/ Reuters), 111 (Banksey/Loop Images), (panda/Daniel J Cox), 119 (tapestry/The Gallery Collection); Dreamstime p.4 (Tokyo at night/Hannamariah), 113 (door handle/ Danace2000), (rubbish bin/Bornholm), (waste paper bin/ Tootles), (landfill/Jeff Breedlove), 117 (flooded house/ Olivier); Fareshare Southwest p.61 (van); Getty Images pp.4 (Mosquito/Geoff du Feu/Taxi), 4 (Colourful toys/ Michael Lander/Nordic Photos), 8 (Family watching TV, 1950s/Keystone/Hulton Archive), 9 (TV/LWA), 12 (Obama), (snow/2011 AFP), (Old lady/Elisabeth L Homelet), (lion/Joel Sartore), 14 (couple/Anna Bryukhanova), 17 (chef/Mike Powell), 22 (Rebecca Hosking/Bloomberg), 30 (computer/ Jim Cotier), 32 (cybercrime/Ikon Images/Magictorch), 40 (Jamie Archer/Simon Joyner), 47 (Leonardo di Caprio/ WireImage), 48 (exam paper/Stockbyte), 50 (Students passing note in class/Keith Brofsky/UpperCut Images), 50 (crib note in pencil case/DigitalVision), 51 (Student using phone in class/Steve Smith/Photographer's Choice), 52 (home-schooling/Paul Bradbury), 58 (demonstration/ Greg Wahl-Stephens/Stringer), 60 (freegan/AFP), 62 (Teen girl portrait/Siri Stafford), 63 (Protesters/G. Brad Lewis/ Stone), 66 (surf/Nacivet), 77 (Sam Worthington/AFP), 79 (Sculpture titled Horse by Fernando Botero/Christopher Furlong), 83 (Tate Modern, London/Justin Lightley), 87 (opera singer/Comstock), 88 (Teens reading magazine/ Leon/Riser), 89 (shop/Huntstock), 92 (canteen food/Yellow Dog Productions), 93 (anti war banner/Greg Wahl-Stephens/Stringer), 96 (TV with static/Thinkstock/ Comstock Images), 97 (Recycling bins/Emma Lee/Life File), 99 (Daily News/2012/Daily News L.p. (New York)), 105 (beach cleaning/Frank & Helena), 106 (Globe/Dieter Spannknebel), 111 (cave painting/G. Dagli Orti), 113 (bus stop/Jasper White), (train/Photographer's Choice), 117 (thermometer/Gallo Images/Neil Overy), 118 (woman in chair/Digital Vision), (make-up artist/Riser), 119 (picture frame), (Easter Island statue/Rich Thompson); Habbo pp.31 (Online game Habbo), 31 (Online game Habbo); iStockphoto pp.16 (Remote control/Terraxplorer), 18 (chocolate/emreogan), 89 (Deodorant/DGID), 89 (Soap/ DNY59), 89 (Bottle of shampoo/Christopher O Driscoll), 96 (Satellite dish/Andy Medina), 96 (Radio waves/Andrey Prokhorov), 96 (Binary code/geopaul), 105 (tree planting/ Nnehring), 113 (football pitch/Arpad Benedek), (black bag/ Jean-Francois Vermette), (wheelie bins/Brian Pamphilon), 115 (microphone/Jean-Francois Vermette), (drum kit/M I S H A), (amp/Don Nichols), (speakers/Geoffrey Holman), (trumpet/group), (bass guitar/Don Bayley), 117 (ice flow/ Alexander Hafemann), 118 (cameraman/otolE), 119 (vase/ Nina Ricci Fedotova); John Clem Clarke p.103 (Cola Billboard by John Clem Clarke/John Clem Clarke with kind permission from Trillion Clarke); Jupiter Images p.38 (Johansson/Sipa Press), 91 (Group of teenagers/ Pixland), 113 (rubbish sorting/getty), 118 (fashion designer/ corbis); Kobal Collection pp.73 (The Dark Knight film poster/Warner Bros/DC Comics), 77 (Avatar/20th Century Fox Film Corporation), 94 (The Day the Earth Stood Still/ Twentieth Century-Fox Film Corporation), 94 (Twilight/ Maverick Films), 94 (Mamma Mia/Universal/Playtone), 110 (Quantum of Solace/Columbia/Danjaq/Eon), 110 (Gandhi/Columbia/Goldcrest); Landov pp.10 & 11 (Kid Nation); London Features International p.47 (Angelina Jolie); Mark Wallinger/Anthony Reynolds Gallery p.82 (A still from the film Sleeper by Mark Wallkinger); MiniclipSA p.90 (screengrab); Mary Beeze p.27 (festival skyscrapers); Naturepl p.101 (coral reef/Constantinos Petrinos); Myspace. com (music screengrab); NI Syndication pp.58 (Protester), 93 (Protests/The Times); Oscilloscope Pictures p.20 (poster); Oxford University Press pp.18 (Carton of juice/Mark Mason), 44 (teenagers on stairs), 49 (friends/Digital Vision), 50 (Student cheating in exam/Rayman/Digital Vision), 52 (Student portrait), 90 (screengrab); Photolibrary p.6 (Teenage girl with shopping bags/Amanaimages), 19 (presents/Alex Schmies), 36 (computer hacker/Simon Belcher), 67 (canteen/Ulrike Preuss), (bully/Leah Warkentin), 108 (New lealand scenery/Chad Ehlers), (sheep/Mula Eshet); Photostage pp.87 (Henry 1V); Press Association Images pp.22 (Modbury bag/Tom Palmer), 43 (David &Victoria/AP), 109 (Police Comic Relief passing out parade/Michael Stephens/PA Archive); Regis Madec/ thaiworldview.com p.53 (Thai school students); Reuters Pictures pp.37 (BMX bikers/Yves Herman), 37 (BMX race/ Stefano Rellandini), 93 (Protests/Nicky Loh); Regis Madec/ thaiworldview.com p.53 (Thai school); Reuters pp.37 (7 BMX racers/Yves Herman), (6 BMX racers/Stefano Rellandini), 93 (anti- smoking placard/Nicky Loh); Rex Features pp.15 (eurostar/Albanpix Ltd), 20 (Colin Beavan/ Everett Collection), 21 (kiwi/Organic Picture Library), 27 (mud/Mark Large/Associated Newspapers), 38 (Scarlett Johannson/Sipa Press), 38 (Daniel Craig/Masatoshi Okauchi), 42 (Brit School/Nick Cunard), (Barack Obama), 46 (Beyonce Knowles/Alex J. Berliner/BEI), 62 (whale hunting/Sinopix), 79 (Banksy/Anna Schoenborn), 82 (Shedboatshed/Simon Starling/The Modern Institute), 107 (seventeen/Startraks Photo), 109 (Sport Relief runners/ David Fisher); Ronald Grant Archive pp.70 (Laurel and Hardy poster/HAL ROACH), 71 (Old film poster), 71 (Black and white film projection), 72 &76 (Catcher in the Rye/ AFP); Scala London pp.81 (Object (Le dejeuner en fourrure), 1936, Oppenheim, Meret (1913-1985)/Digital image, The Museum of Modern Art, New York/Scala, Florence), 103 (Pollock, Jackson (1912-1956), Autumn Rhythm (Number 30), 1950 New York/The Metropolitan Museum of Art/Art Resource/Scala, Florence); Science Photo Library p.4 (Platinum nugget/E.R.Degginger); Shutterstock pp.18 (Toilet paper/Konstantin Yolshin), 18 (Packet of crisps/Ewa Walicka), 18 (Jar of coffee), 29 (students/Dean Mitchell), 89 (Tube of toothpaste), 107 (Adele/Featureflash), 107 (Bruno Mars/DFree), 107 (Katy Perry/Helga Esteb), 107 (One Direction/Mr Pics), 107 (Rihanna/s_buckley), 113 (keys/Doug Stevens), (recycle bins/prism68), (bin/Neale Cousland/View Portfolio)115 (keyboards/Nikita Rogul); Simon Starling/The Modern Institute p.82 (Shedboatshed by Simon Starling/Anthony Reynolds Gallery); Sotheby's p.78 (Claude Monet 1840-1926, The Nympheas); Still Pictures p.22 (turtle/Pierre Huguet/BIOphoto), 117 (logging/ Martin Harvey), (dry earth); Superstock pp.87 (street performer/Age Fotostock), 119 (mosaic/Age Fotostock); Wikipedia p.98 (screen grabs); Tomma Abts/Greegrassi, London p.82 (Tomma Abts Ebe, 2005), London © DACS 2010; White Cube p.82 (Damien Hirst Mother and Child Divided 1993/Stephen White Courtesy White Cube/ copyright Damien Hurst); www.eppingforest.gov.uk p.97 (Local Agenda logo); Yes! Magazine p.21 (Colin Beavan/ Paul Dunn), Pa Photos p.41 (crowd/Gareth Fuller); White Cube p.82 (Damien Hirst Mother and Child Divided 1993/ Stephen White Courtesy White Cube/© Hirst Holdings Limited and Damien Hirst. All rights reserved, DACS 2010).

Although every effort has been made to trace and contact copyright holders before publication, this has not been possible in some cases. We apologise for any apparent infringement of copyright and, if notified, the publisher will be pleased to rectify any errors or omissions at the earliest possible opportunity.